Overcoming Common Problems

Overcoming Gambling

A guide for problem and compulsive gamblers

PHILIP MAWER

sheldon **PRESS**

First published in Great Britain in 2010

Sheldon Press
36 Causton Street
London SW1P 4ST
www.sheldonpress.co.uk

British Library Cataloguing-in-Publication Data
A catalogue record for this book is available from the British Library

ISBN 978-1-84709-099-7

1 3 5 7 9 10 8 6 4 2

Typeset by Fakenham Photosetting Ltd, Fakenham, Norfolk
Printed in Great Britain by Ashford Colour Press

Produced on paper from sustainable forests

Contents

Preface: For gamblers and their loved ones   vii

Introduction: Are you ready to stop gambling?   1

Part One: Stopping

  1 Phases of problem gambling   14

  2 Simply a habit: breaking the fear and mythology of
      gambling   18

  3 The Release: creating the 'rock bottom'   24

  4 Gamblers Aloud   39

Part Two: Staying stopped

  5 The illness   46

  6 Signposts: dealing with urges   56

  7 Restoring your dignity and self-respect   66

  8 The chip of change   71

  9 The futility and danger of gambling   77

 10 The importance of humility and compassion   86

 11 Where your money went! Anchoring your hatred of the
      gambling industry   94

 12 Cruel facts about a cruel industry   98

 13 Life after gambling   102

Appendix   106

Useful addresses and references   110

Index   114

Dedicated to my darling wife for all she has been through, and to all those family members, friends, partners and spouses for all they will go through during the recovery process and for all they've been through prior to Creating the Rock Bottom.

Preface
For gamblers and their loved ones

'Though no one can go back and make a brand new start, anyone can start from now and make a brand new ending.'

Carl Bard

If you as a gambler think that you can simply buy this book, read it and quit gambling, then please put it back on the shelf and continue your gambling-obsessed life. If you are prepared to read it *and* action the key points contained within, then please read on.

The purpose of the questions that follow is to describe what this book is about, how and whom it can help, and how the system it outlines was created. I say system because the chances are that as a gambler you had some private 'system' of your own that you felt helped you win, especially in the early phases of your gambling (see Chapter 1, Phases of problem gambling). This book aims to replace some of that 'gambling thinking' with new, healthy, effective thoughts, and I hope you'll find that the tips and tricks are geared to the gambler's mentality and thought patterns.

If you're the partner, friend or parent of a problem gambler, then I sincerely hope this book proves helpful to you. It won't wave a magic wand over your gambler so that he or she never gambles again; nor does it tell you how to conduct your own recovery from living with a gambler. But it does tell you how to work with your gambler at challenging his or her compulsive behaviour – how to confront him or her, how to support his or her efforts to change, and how to overcome the past and move on. Again, you'll find that the system outlined in this book is shaped to the gambler and what can be his or her slippery, convoluted thinking. To pin this down, you need all the help you can get – but so does the gambler!

What is the goal of this book?
Quite simply, to stop you ever gambling again and to help loved ones support you. This isn't really a book for people who just want to cut down on their gambling, though obviously I hope you find it useful if you are concerned in any way about your gambling.

However, the aim is not just to increase the time between relapses or returns to any form of gambling. That to me is failure. Commit, commit and commit again so that you can stop gambling for ever. If that is too far in the future, then why not at least explore if it is possible?

How was this book created?
This book began life as a home-grown therapy created by my wife and me. You will see all the steps carefully explained in each chapter. I worked abroad, away from my wife, so my therapy continued through long telephone calls and emails between us.

Gambling recovery in many ways still remains to be developed. There's scant psychiatric literature and the field is still in its infancy, with research being contradictory and inconclusive. Likewise, support groups operate on fairly rough and ready principles which work well for some people, but not for others. Most of the recovery methods available at present, and most of the 'philosophy' based around recovery, is built on the idea that you just live one gambling-free day of your life at a time. The problem with this, in my opinion, is that it doesn't take the focus off gambling, and seems to make your power over your own life conditional. My aim is to put gambling out of the equation altogether and to hand you back your life totally, at least until you have finished this book. After that, you can decide which method you prefer, and how your future goes!

For me, Gamblers Anonymous wasn't an option; apart from it being difficult to access in a life of constant travelling, its ethos wasn't really for me, as I explain later, though it may well be invaluable for others. The three self-help books I bought over the internet made no sense to me and offered me no firm conviction that I could beat my gambling addiction. I tried using an online chat room, and while it was in some ways initially comforting to see I wasn't the only one with the problem, the harrowing stories people were telling depressed both me and my wife. Furthermore, when I followed other people's online 'recoveries', virtually all of them eventually relapsed back into gambling, or seemed to give up writing their recovery diaries altogether after a couple of days or weeks. I knew that wasn't going to work for me. I had to begin with the total conviction that I could permanently beat compulsive gambling.

As I grew stronger, coming out of what I call the 'gambling coma', we started to realize that I really could put gambling behind me, and that maybe we could pass our methods on to others in order to help them. We started analysing each step of my journey, what we were doing and why it was working. Much of our correspondence became the basis of this system.

I've tried so often before to stop, how is your method different?
'A journey of a thousand miles begins with a single step,' as the ancient Chinese proverb says. Many compulsive gamblers have probably taken that 'single step' on the journey of abstinence or quitting so often that we've probably already walked the first mile, but unfortunately backwards! We are now facing a journey of 1,001 miles or further. How many times have you looked at yourself in the mirror after a devastating run of losses (maybe you call it 'bad luck') and said 'Never again'? Maybe you've gone further and posted your 'confession' on a Stop Gambling website, or even walked into a Gamblers Anonymous meeting, but still you've found yourself back at the tables (whether real or 'virtual') again, or filling out betting slips, or feeding the slots.

I tried countless times to stop myself, until this last time. I'm fairly sure, and I certainly hope, that I will be able to make you understand exactly why you haven't been able to stop, despite trying so often, and why you seem to have so many 'rock bottoms'. You can learn how to create your last 'rock bottom' and immediately start putting yourself in control.

Through this system, I have cleared all my debts, have enough finances to move to an idyllic location and have now embarked on a life of helping others, but do you know what the greatest thing is? I have actually started liking myself again and have started thinking that life really *is* worth living.

You'll note a few differences between our suggestions and the conventional wisdom about giving up gambling. For example, one piece of standard advice is to keep a gambling diary. That's fine if you just want to monitor and assess your gambling, but it doesn't work for the person who's desperate to give up altogether. Some people also find it helpful to write down gambling urges, rather than act upon them. For me, though, a diary really goes against the ethos of this book, which focuses on the present (i.e. today). A diary is the record of the past, which we don't want. Gambling was the past. We want you to live today.

So, instead, we created four key 'signposts', strong visual reminders of your gambling to which you refer occasionally on your journey out of compulsive gambling (see Chapter 6). These include your written gambling history and a printout of bank statements.

Again, conventional wisdom suggests that concerned gamblers limit access to cash – set a gambling budget, get their partner to give them a daily allowance, use cards without PIN numbers, and so on. Likewise, this isn't going to work for the problem gambler who, once he or she starts, has a real compulsion to keep gambling. It's a bit like advising an alcoholic to limit the drinking to one or two tipples a day – controlled indulgence works for some people, but for many, abstinence is the only option. Only about one in five gamblers find it fairly easy to give up, so it is clear that something else is needed.

Is this system only for the compulsive gambler, or also for those affected by the gambling?
This system is for everyone affected by compulsive gambling. I constantly refer to the compulsive gambler's loved ones, be they spouse, partner, parent or friend, how gambling may have affected them, and how the cessation of gambling may affect them. To help you both assess how severe the gambling problem is, see the checklist of questions in the Introduction. Then read on to see the best way to help the compulsive gambler. Trust me, it isn't all tea and biscuits and a shoulder to cry on for the compulsive gambler – far from it.

Were you really a compulsive gambler?

I was a compulsive gambler who, with loving support from my wife, was completely cured of what I consider to be a hugely destructive social evil. At 45, having worked and lived almost continually overseas for the past 15 years, on a large salary with bonuses, with none of my own children to raise and educate, what did I have to my name, at the end of my gambling career? Approximately £40,000 of debt, no house, no car, no savings, no pension, no life insurance, no health insurance and at times not even enough money in the bank to pay for the contents of a shopping trolley. The very least that I gambled away in the 27 years of my 'adult' life is £350,000, and I would put the figure at closer to £400,000. Properly invested in property, shares and high deposit accounts, by rights I should now be a millionaire at the very least. Financial amounts mean nothing and are relative to each individual, so that is the last time you will see them mentioned in such detail. Only you as the compulsive gambler know how bad financially your gambling has got so far.

Is this book an autobiography of your gambling?
No, not at all! This book *isn't* about me, because you don't care about me; you care about yourself, and how you are going to get out of compulsive gambling. I understand that. If you're a desperate gambler, all I ask of you is to trust me enough to accept that I have been where you are today. If you want to know more about me and my time gambling, then go to <www.gamblersaloud.com>.

However, I do want you to know that I've felt that hatred of myself and the world, that blind despair at the unfairness of it all. You need to know I've looked in the mirror a thousand times and made those promises to myself, *'Never again'*, and then heard the devil's voice whisper in my ear, 'I know you said never again, but the favourite in the 3.30 p.m. at Kempton is a cert and at good odds, so you could at least get back on it what you lost yesterday.' I've felt the pain of wondering where the house rent is going to come from this month, how you'll repay your brother what you promised, or how you'll lie to your beloved wife, just one more time, about where this month's salary went. You need to know that I've been with you, with that rush when you've fixed another score, borrowed another £100 or found another £1,000 credit card. I've stared into my mother's eyes and lied to feed this monster inside me. I've breathed those minutes with that hot money in your hand as you've planned 'the great escape'. I've trudged those lonely streets, after the last roulette spin landed on the number before yours, on your last £5 chip, and you were left wondering 'What will I do, where will I go?' I've driven that bookie's pen deeply, silently, excruciatingly into the back of my hand, as I've heard my horse lose a steward's inquiry which would have given me the final piece of my winning Yankee.

I've been there. I've sold the T-shirt. It was all I had left.

Is your aim to ban gambling?
No! I'm not that naive or unrealistic. What I want to do is help all those people for whom gambling has become compulsive or even 'just' problematic, whose lives it has probably taken over in the most negative of ways, and who have the commitment to know they can cure themselves.

In a perfect world, everyone would be intelligent enough – and compassionate enough – never to actually want to gamble, so the entire industry would naturally dry up. In a perfect world, no one could possibly lay £10 on the roll of a dice, the turn of a card or the speed of a horse, while somewhere else in the world a child lies starving, a dog dies abandoned, or a teenage cancer patient passes quietly away through lack of a cure.

But hey, that would be a perfect world, wouldn't it?

Introduction
Are you ready to stop gambling?

Now it's crunch time, when you need to decide whether you are 'in' or 'out', in terms of giving up gambling totally. If you are close to someone you think may have a serious gambling problem, by the end of this introduction you should have a much clearer idea of the nature of the problem. You should also have a better understanding of what both you and the compulsive gambler will face once he or she stops gambling.

The following 20-point checklist, produced by Gamblers Anonymous (GA), is designed to help gamblers decide whether or not they have a problem:

- Do you lose time from work due to gambling?
- Is gambling making your home life unhappy?
- Is gambling affecting your reputation?
- Have you ever felt remorse after gambling?
- Do you ever gamble to get money with which to pay debts or otherwise solve financial difficulties?
- Does gambling cause a decrease in your ambition and efficiency?
- After losing, do you feel you must return as soon as possible and win back your losses?
- After a win, do you have a strong urge to return and win more?
- Do you often gamble until your last pound is gone?
- Do you ever borrow to finance your gambling?
- Have you ever sold anything to finance your gambling?
- Are you reluctant to use gambling money for normal expenditures?
- Does gambling make you careless of the welfare of your family?
- Do you gamble longer than you planned?
- Do you ever gamble to escape worry or trouble?
- Have you ever committed, or considered committing, an illegal act to finance gambling?
- Does gambling cause you to have difficulty in sleeping?

- Do arguments, disappointments or frustrations create an urge within you to gamble?
- Do you have an urge to celebrate any good fortune by a few hours' gambling?
- Have you ever considered self-destruction as a result of your gambling?

GA state that most compulsive gamblers answer yes to at least seven of the above points. Honestly now, how many did you tick? Read them one more time and then think carefully.

If you answered yes to just one of those points, then surely there is no point in your continuing to gamble.

Checklist for partners or friends

As it's often hard as compulsive gamblers (hopefully in your case, soon to be ex-compulsive gamblers) for us to be completely honest with ourselves, I'm now going to include a list of 20 telltale signs to help partners or friends recognize if there is a problem. I will refer to potential compulsive gamblers as 'he' throughout this list, but of course women as well as men may be compulsive gamblers:

- Has he become distant and almost unaware of your presence sometimes when he is around you?
- Does he appear to lack concentration or interest in your attempts at conversation with him?
- Does he have surprising mood swings on returning home, totally different from the mood he left the house in?
- Do you think he is having an affair?
- Are you often wondering why there never seems to be enough money even for the basics?
- Similarly, do you sometimes wonder where the money for surprise gifts, or unexpected nights out (or even holidays), has come from, when only a few days ago there was nothing?
- Does he seem keen to run errands for you, or even to be exercising more than he used to, and yet not appear to be getting any fitter?
- Has he lost interest in sex and/or does he have trouble sleeping?
- Does he use the computer at home a lot and appear agitated

when you interrupt him, or do you see the screen suddenly change when you approach?

- Does he take longer than you would expect to go shopping or take the car to a car wash?
- Have you ever found small pens in his pockets?
- Does he hide bank statements or credit card statements from you, and/or is he nervous when the postman delivers, always wanting to get to the mail first?
- If you do see bank/credit card statements, are there entries (either debits or credits) that you don't understand and have to ask about?
- Is he working late continually or going in, supposedly to the office, at weekends for seemingly no noticeable financial benefit (i.e. overtime, etc.)?
- Does he spend longer than you would expect reading the daily newspaper?
- Are you aware he gambles and do you ever go to a casino or race meeting with him?
- Have you ever confronted him about his gambling but accept his reassurance that he has everything under control?
- If you are aware of his gambling, does he ever tell you about his losses, or only his wins?
- Does he appear nervous when friends or family call unexpectedly?
- Have friends or family recently been acting differently towards either of you, or staying away more than they used to?

My wife could have ticked all 20 of those before she finally confronted me, as we will see in Chapter 3, so partners or friends need to take a good long look at the list, in order to decide when or how to begin. If as a compulsive gambler you are reading this part, then you need to know that you probably aren't being that clever about hiding your gambling, and so you either have a choice to come clean or be rumbled.

The gambler's loved ones

Because compulsive gamblers also tend to be compulsive liars, as a partner, parent or friend, you have to steel yourself and teach yourself how to rumble the lies and confront your loved ones with them. Gamblers lie in order to obtain money to gamble. They lie in order to hide their losses. They lie to hide their winnings, or to hide the time spent gambling. They lie to hide their emotions; in fact there becomes nothing about which they won't lie, if it helps to protect their 'mistress' or 'lover', gambling.

The life of lies you may discover if your partner is a compulsive gambler can be devastating. All I can say is, try not to take it personally, however ineffectual that sounds. Your partner wasn't lying to you and everyone else in order to hurt you, but was driven by a monster that had to be fed, just as a heroin addict must feed the dragon inside. You may well not understand right now why your partner couldn't simply stop, but that is the same for any addiction. The pain of trying to understand is so much greater and the ability to comprehend so much lesser in gambling, because the addict isn't feeding his or her body with anything physical. The body isn't becoming addicted to any actual substance, as it is with nicotine, alcohol or hard drugs (although some researchers have speculated that gamblers become addicted to changes in the brain that take place during the excitement of gambling, when levels of dopamine, a chemical associated with feelings of reward, increase).

For now, though, what all these lies may do to you is make you doubt yourself. You may doubt your own intelligence for not having spotted earlier what's going on. You may doubt your judgement. You'll almost certainly doubt your love for your partner, and he may doubt his love for you, in that he had to find fulfilment in the arms of another – gambling. It is very possible you will feel dirty, almost violated – some people come to view gambling as their partner's lover or mistress, and feel deeply betrayed and shocked at the realization that, all along, the gambling partner has in fact been intimate both with you and with a whole gambling life of whose extent you were probably unaware (particularly if they were hooked on online gambling).

It's likely that you won't easily trust your partner again, and possibly you won't openly trust others as you used to, for fear of being caught out again. It's very common to feel betrayed not only by your partner, but by everyone from whom he borrowed money to fuel his gambling. Gamblers are often able to ensure that their partners aren't told of any loans, something which compromises or even destroys the relationship between the non-gambling partner and those who lent the compulsive gambler money.

In practical financial terms, you may well have your own credit rating affected if the money your partner used for gambling came from a joint account. If you default on the mortgage because of gambling debts, it won't just be the compulsive gambler who is evicted from the property. It will be you and your children, if you have them, also.

Many partners themselves seek solace in the bottle or in drugs in order to overcome the negative emotions described above. Some harm themselves, or seek comfort in the arms of others, in order to pay the compulsive gambler back a fraction of the pain he or she has caused. Of course, this won't solve anything, natural though it may be. And sadly, some relationships don't survive. However, it may help if you bear in mind that many compulsive gamblers are big on self-destruction and low in self-esteem. Hurtful behaviour from a partner is only likely to enhance those two strong drives, rather than resolving the gambling. This isn't to bully the partner into compliance with the gambling – far from it. Setting boundaries is an essential part of supporting the gambler, as you will see.

The main thing is to try and maintain your belief in yourself and in your relationship. Try and imagine how strong you, as the partner of a compulsive gambler, will feel if you can endure all this and still come out the other side with your marriage and/or love intact and your partner cured and back to the wonderful, caring, generous person you fell for in the first place.

Preparing for the fray

If you are the compulsive gambler, then maybe the first healing rays of light are penetrating the fog of your gambling coma as you begin to realize the devastation your gambling has wrought on those you love. You may need to stand up to a tsunami of anger, hatred, frustration and pain, so steel yourself now and be strong. If you are alone and have no partner, then you must prepare for the battle that will rage in your head between the part of you that wants to give up gambling for ever and the part that wants to destroy you.

It is very similar to having someone sitting across a table from you, willing you to stop, but it is all kept inside you.

Unfortunately, the pain isn't over once the dam bursts and your gambling is out in the open. For a while, the treatment is going to hurt a lot more than the illness, but hang on in there.

If you are the non-gambler, you may well be sickened at the scale of the problem and wonder where (and indeed if) you are going to find the strength to pull through it, and come out the other side. You may be thinking, 'Isn't it just easier to walk away and let the gambler rot in the hell he or she created?' While only you can be the judge of this, try to disassociate the gambler from the gambling. Make it plain you will support the person, but not the addiction. The following steps may help:

- If you think there is a problem, state what you have observed calmly, but without (if possible) getting into heated arguments which give the gambler a chance to be defensive.
- Tell the gambler you care and are willing to stand by him or her, but that changes have to take place. Make it plain that if he or she doesn't change or seek help, you will take action, for example by asking him or her to leave. (See Chapter 3, 'The Release', for more on how to confront a problem gambler.)
- If necessary, take steps to protect your finances, visiting banks and financial advisors to find out your rights and responsibilities. I hope, once you've read this book, that it won't be necessary!
- Don't loan the gambler money, or pay his or her gambling debts. This may sound harsh, but the gambler has to come to terms with reality at some point.
- Inform yourself about problem gambling and try to understand how the gambler's mind works – read this book.

What do I have to lose or gain by giving up gambling?

This is something you should sit down and discuss with your nearest and dearest. If this is not appropriate, then write it down and come back to it later. Partners and friends need to say exactly what they will do if the compulsive gambler doesn't quit, literally, today. We have drawn up a diagram, the Ladder of Life (see Figure 1.1), which may help you sum up your situation right now.

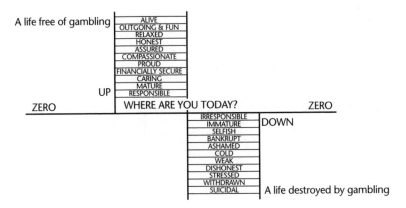

Figure 1.1 The Ladder of Life – the author's situation

The Ladder of Life is a simple exercise designed for both the gambler and his or her partner to spend a little reflective time on seeing where the gambling problem is taking them (the Down part of the ladder) and where a non-gambling life could take them (the Up part). It is similar in some ways to the Tree of Humility (see Chapter 10) and is designed to get both parties to discuss the issue together, or, if the gambler has no partner, to help think hard about where the gambling is taking him or her. The example in Figure 1.1 shows how we saw my situation, but you should do your own; this is why we have included a blank version (Figure 1.2) for you to copy and complete. Think about questions such as the following:

- Which ladder do I really want to take – Up or Down?
- Am I still arrogant and stupid enough to think I can control my gambling?
- Am I going to regret not taking action now?
- If I am, say, four rungs down the Down ladder can I still climb to Zero and then begin the Up ladder?

Fill in the Down part of the ladder by adding words that describe how you feel at the moment, and how you think your life will be if you carry on gambling. Fill in the Up part by adding words that describe how you would like to feel having stopped gambling, and how your life will have improved.

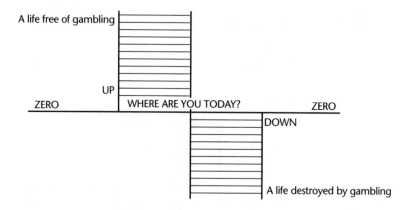

Figure 1.2 The Ladder of Life – to copy and complete

Let's do it!

Throughout my life, I've read numerous self-help books, biographies and autobiographies, particularly those of successful business people. I know that gambling sucked the lifeblood of ambition out of me, and for the first 25 years of my adult life, none of my dreams were truly realized. That is a cruel waste of the prime years of life and it is where a lot of my anger towards gambling comes from. (See Chapter 11, 'Where your money went!', for more on how to harness anger and make it work for you so that you don't gamble again.)

One common theme in many books written by successful people is simply getting on with it. They urge you not to look at the end, or the pain in the middle, as you battle against the odds to fulfil your dream – just look at today and get on with it. Having a great idea is one thing, but the execution of the idea is what will make it a success. However, right now, if you are a compulsive gambler, you probably cannot envisage the end – a time when gambling is no longer part (or indeed all) of your life; a time when you unconditionally enjoy the love and respect of your partner, your children, your family and friends; a time where you are financially and emotionally secure; a time where you have purpose and meaning in your life. Am I right?

If you find looking to the End is too far, you may begin looking at the middle. That is a time that in your mind is filled with pain, a time that will be spent confronting banks, possibly employers and loved ones, and trying to turn your life around and rebuild a future for yourself. Have I captured at least some of the fears you experience when you look at The Middle? I'm sure I have. But I can almost guarantee that if you *continue* to gamble, then every one of the above, and probably more besides, will happen to you. Read the list again and think of your own reasons and honestly ask yourself, how many times have you thought that is what is going to happen to you if you continue gambling? I know I did. So here you are now, presenting to yourself all the reasons why you shouldn't totally give up gambling. In fact they are exactly the reasons why you should give up! How can you not give up, faced with such overwhelming logic?

Why we procrastinate

Did you know that we do more to avoid pain than we do to pursue pleasure? All this means is that most of us (gamblers and non-gamblers alike) would rather bumble along in our humdrum, boring life than risk going after what we would really enjoy, because we might suffer the pain of failure or rejection along the way. This probably helps explain how people become stuck in the gambling routine, and why they may procrastinate about change, even when they know that it will improve life beyond recognition.

For compulsive gamblers this so-called pleasure and pain principle (or just pleasure principle) holds especially true. Although we know our compulsive gambling is causing pain both to us and those we love, we are sure that stopping gambling is going to cause us and those we love (particularly if they don't know the extent of the problem) even more pain. And so we continue to gamble. We believe that if we could stop gambling altogether, then we would eventually find pleasure, but we are too scared of inflicting more pain on ourselves and others to reach that pleasure by stopping.

What you, the compulsive gambler, need to draw strength from at this early stage is that not stopping gambling out of fear of causing pain (to yourself and others) is no different from 'normal' people being too scared to change jobs or ask for a promotion, get out of an unhappy relationship, begin a diet or rigorous exercise, move house, or any of the other things that can keep 'normal' people from living the lives they dreamed of. My point is that we compulsive gamblers suffer from a similar affliction to that which affects 'normal' people, and that is: procrastination.

For the gambler's partner, it may also take effort to bite the bullet. Non-gambling partners and friends need to try and recognize that, fundamentally, most compulsive gamblers are good people who can kick their addiction but who need help, support and advice. Think of all the times you have wanted to do something, or make a major change in your life, and have been too scared to do it. You may even have wanted to confront your partner about his or her gambling in the past, but have been too scared to, or too scared of the 'fallout', and so have let it go. In other words, you may be able to understand and empathize more if you bear in mind that you too may have gone through the same kind of dilemmas as your compulsive gambling partner. If you can find it in your heart to show a little sympathy at this early stage, it will go a long way to beginning the journey of healing your loved one of his or her illness.

Do you need a health professional?

Partners and families, and sometimes gamblers themselves, sometimes wonder if they need professional help, such as a psychologist or counsellor who specializes in addiction. It's a good idea to get professional help if the gambler:

- has a history of serious mental illness, such as depression or bipolar disorder;
- has another problem, such as alcohol abuse or drug addiction;
- talks about suicide, or has made previous suicide attempts;
- becomes very angry and/or displays physical violence.

Equally, if you are the partner of a gambler and you feel you just can't cope on your own, bear in mind that you may need therapy too in your own right. Start with your family doctor, or contact the British Association of Counselling and Psychotherapy (<www.bacp.co.uk>, or see Useful addresses).

Are you ready for this?

In conclusion, this is the point where you are standing at the edge of the bridge wondering whether to do your first bungee jump! If you are the compulsive gambler, then you may well have confirmed what you already knew. You have an out-of-control problem that you really want to put a stop to, but which you haven't been able to every time you've tried in the past. You've read up to this point and now you need to decide:

- Do I put the book down, think about it, feel mildly good about myself for at least buying the book, promise myself I'll carry on reading it, get distracted and then go off and gamble again?
- Do I say, 'What a load of rubbish, this guy must have been lucky to quit gambling, I'm doomed to failure'?
- Or do I read on, take the actions suggested, and come out of the closet about my gambling, convinced I can beat it this time?

You need to give it some careful thought, because this is a life-changing moment for you. It's probably more of a challenge than gambling – in fact, the gambling may not have challenged you for a long time, if ever. Trying to pay the bills and buy food isn't a challenge even if you have thrown everything away gambling. Tapping up another friend, relative or credit card company for more money to gamble with isn't a challenge. Lying to your partner about your gambling isn't a challenge. This is a challenge. Not just 'giving it a go' to see if it works. Not just trying it to see if you can limit or control your gambling. But truly committing yourself to stop gambling for ever.

It's understandable if this causes mental pain – indeed, you may well have reached the point where it's painful to continue gambling, painful to stop. You may also feel that your pain is multiplied by guilt at the distress gambling has caused your family and friends. The good news is that if you feel even a shred of guilt, there is hope. The guilt is a sign of the essential decency within your soul, and as long as you have this then you can turn the page and begin this journey.

If you are the partner of a compulsive gambler, then it is decision time for you also. I hope I've given you some insight into what is in store if you decide to continue, and to stick by your compulsive gambler as we progress through this book. Please be assured that the book doesn't leave you at this point. You are integral to the success of healing the compulsive gambler, so this book is also aimed at helping you every step of the way.

To an outsider, compulsive gambling merely consists of the selfish, immature antics of people who care only about themselves and who are only interested in the 'buzz' or high – although most compulsive gamblers are past the point where gambling is enjoyable or they are chasing any form of high.

Whatever your decision, if you read on a little more, you'll learn that compulsive gamblers aren't in it for any form of enjoyment. The vast majority of them are miserable, and gambling feeds that misery.

Part One
STOPPING

1

Phases of problem gambling

Before embarking on the recovery system it is essential to take a little time honestly to appraise where you think you are with your gambling. The fact that you or your partner have bought this book highlights the possibility that you have the makings of a problem, if you don't already have a full-blown crisis.

There have been several studies of the various phases of problematic or compulsive gambling, and a consensus that the course runs very similar to that of drug or alcohol addiction. Briefly, the phases are:

- winning
- losing
- desperation
- helplessness

In more detail the phases can be seen like this.

The winning phase

This tends to follow a characteristic pattern. At first an occasional bet leads to some small wins. These wins lead the occasional gambler into a feeling that she has a 'system', a lucky number, or an almost failsafe way of picking a winner. She begins increasing her stakes, and as the stakes are increased so the wins become larger. The gambler will become more and more vocal about such wins and display arrogance to friends who slog away to earn in a week what she has earned from a three-minute race or a 15-second roll of a roulette wheel. Depending on the character of the gambler, this phase can last anywhere from months to years.

Are you in the winning phase?

It is unlikely you are, as people in this phase typically think that they can win at gambling, don't have a problem, are in control, and therefore are the last people in the world who need this system.

If you are in the winning phase, ask yourself whether you really are 'the chosen one', the person who broke the bank at Monte Carlo, the one who really could become a pro. Then ask yourself whether there's a possibility that you have just had a couple of lucky breaks but know deep down that your luck can't continue.

We will be doing some serious reflection on this in a later chapter, but for now, have an honest think and give yourself an honest answer: why not just stop now? Don't let yourself put this book down and then look back in a year or five years, when you are in one of the later phases, and think 'why couldn't I have quit while I was still in the winning phase?'

The losing phase

Pretty much as night follows day, so the losing phase follows the winning phase. If it didn't, then there wouldn't be any phases at all, as there would be no forms of gambling available. The gambling industry is there for one reason and one reason only, and that is to take as much of your money as it can. If everyone wins and they have to give back more of their money than they've taken of yours, they go out of business. Almost too obvious to say, but true. The losing phase typically follows this pattern:

The gambler is often shocked to be on a long losing streak and this affects her mentality as much as her bank balance. For example, she may think, 'Hang on a sec – I'm a winner not a loser. I'm the one everyone in the casino/bookmaker's admired and envied with those big wins, I can't have them sniggering at me with these continual losses.'

Her pride is taking a kicking so she fights back. She becomes angry and irrational and raises her bets in the hope of raising her winnings and recovering her losses. She changes her betting patterns and might go high stakes on low odds in the hope of winning something. She might even try high stakes at high odds as she becomes more desperate.

Her financial situation worsens by the day and her work suffers. That further increases her stress, so her relationships suffer. The downward spiral has begun. As the stress increases, so her personality changes. She often becomes withdrawn, irritable and doesn't appear to be 'there' in a conversation. 'The lights are on, but no one's in.' She is totally preoccupied either with gambling, or with funding gambling.

Are you in the losing phase?

If you are, then that's great! You have the greatest chance of recovery. Any arrogance from the winning phase will have been well and truly knocked out of you, you'll be becoming desperate and you still have the sense to seek help.

Again, do lots of reflection *now* so you can accept that you are in this phase and you need help. Please don't think you can use the system to help yourself out of the losing phase and back into the winning phase, because it doesn't work like that.

Think back to the person you were, even before the winning phase, and look at the person you are now. See what gambling is doing to you and those around you. Commit yourself now to returning to your former self. Don't worry about how. Just commit to getting back there and we'll make it happen.

The desperation phase

In this phase the funds really are starting to dry up. The gambler has probably remortgaged his house, maxed out his credit cards, blown his savings and gambled away any money given by friends and family supposedly to pay bills and keep him afloat. The gambler may well now be resorting to illegal methods to fund his gambling.

His stakes and gambling patterns are even more desperate than they were in the losing phase, as the hole he is in is now so much deeper. That means that what would have previously been a big win will now barely scratch the surface of his debts. He needs a lottery-sized win to get him out of trouble.

Many people call this the 'rock bottom' stage, but you'll see that we take a different, and we feel, a stronger, more positive approach, whereby we 'create' your rock bottom. By doing that you don't have to wait to get to the desperation phase or, worse, the helplessness stage.

Are you in the desperation phase?

If you are, it's still OK as you should be very receptive to (in fact desperate for) offers of help, so you should be able to listen to this book's message, and absorb the suggestions.

Try to clear your head of the difficulties your gambling has created around you. This book shows you how to go back to friends and family members, and hopefully bring them back into the fold to help not just you yourself, but also them, through your recovery. It isn't too late for you to recover totally from this, so let's get on with it now!

The helplessness phase

By now there is every possibility the gambler has, at the very least, had suicidal thoughts and may even have attempted suicide. Frequently she is suffering from a co-addiction, typically alcohol. She is almost continually in a depressive and resigned state of mind. Due to the fact that everything else around her has collapsed (relationships, jobs, security, etc.), she is literally waiting for her own collapse.

Are you in the helplessness phase?

Don't give up. You can still pull through this. There are people out there who love you and can help you. It's going to take a lot of strength and pain, but you are going through a lot of pain now. So for once you have nothing to lose.

2

Simply a habit: breaking the fear and mythology of gambling

Research into problem gambling is still in its early stages. After I stopped gambling, I searched for scientific information on why people gamble and, in particular, why some people become compulsive gamblers. Given the increasing scale of the problem, there was worryingly little material available, and absolutely nothing that gave me a moment of understanding whereby I could state categorically, 'Yes, that was why I became a compulsive gambler.' Problem gambling is categorized by some as an impulse control disorder, by others as an addiction. However, while more research is being undertaken into how it might be classified as an illness, there's still disagreement as to how it should be defined. More to the point, the labelling doesn't necessarily help the person trapped in the problem, as so many gambling addicts and their families know to their cost.

For the time being, let's see if it's helpful to look at gambling in terms of another addiction, such as smoking. Compare the following questions, which with just a little alteration could be asked of both addicted smokers and addicted gamblers:

Smoking	*Gambling*
Are you addicted to filling your lungs with poisonous chemicals?	Are you addicted to burning £50 notes?
Are you happy about your deteriorating health?	Are you happy about your deteriorating health?
Do you really enjoy smoking?	Do you really enjoy gambling?
Do you enjoy being a social outcast?	Do you enjoy how much time you spend gambling and not being with your family/friends?

Are you happy spending money on cigarettes rather than on more enjoyable activities?	Are you happy spending money on gambling rather than on more enjoyable activities?
Do you encourage your children to smoke?	Do you encourage your children to gamble?
If you were given a second chance at life would you still take up smoking?	If you were given a second chance at life would you still take up gambling?

I could go on. But I'm sure you get the point, and I'm equally sure that the answer from every smoker and gambler asked those questions would be the same: no. You could probably also ask an alcoholic a similar set of questions. So the conclusion is that smokers and gamblers (and alcoholics) are addicted to something that they basically hate doing (or if they still think they enjoy doing it, then they hate the effects of their activity), and that, given a choice, they would stop altogether. The great news is that you now have that choice, if you are a compulsive gambler, by reading this book and following our system.

A quick but important note here with regard to phrasing. If you accept the above statement, that we are addicted to doing something we actually hate doing, or its effects, then let's never describe stopping that activity as 'giving it up'. That sounds as if we are sacrificing something we enjoy, or that we are going to go through hardship by no longer being allowed to do it. From here onwards, we celebrate the fact that we can no longer gamble. We pity those who still gamble and we try where we can to help them, once we are strong enough ourselves.

The next question is, if we're addicted to something we hate doing, why can't we simply stop? A question a lot of people closest to me asked, and something that they too could never understand. If it isn't the action of gambling itself that is addictive or enjoyable (as with smokers not actually liking the taste of cigarettes or alcoholics not enjoying the taste of whisky), then what is it?

The twilight zone

For many gambling addicts, it's the state of mind they're in while gambling that they became addicted to.

Tom

When I was gambling, in any form, be it in a bookmaker's, at a race track, in a casino or logged on to an internet gaming site, I entered a 'twilight zone' in my mind. It was rather like a trance in that the real world was blocked out, and all my stresses and pressures, problems and issues were put to one side. I focused on the form page, the running of a race, the spin of a wheel, turn of a card or roll of a dice, and nothing else mattered.

Are you the same as Tom? Mentally now, take a breather from this book, and imagine yourself gambling. Isn't everything else temporarily blotted out? Your heart races a little faster at the pounding of the horses' hooves or the tinkling of the roulette ball, and then it is all over. Either you lost or you won, but you must try again, and meanwhile everything outside your gambling world is on hold. If you can relate to this, then you've taken a big step towards understanding how gambling took hold of you.

What happens while you are gambling is that you are 'transported' out of the real world and into a fantasy world or 'twilight zone'. A world, however temporary, where it doesn't matter that the rent isn't paid, the car isn't fixed, the promotion at work isn't achieved, the boyfriend/girlfriend isn't satisfied, the illness isn't cured, the ambitions aren't fulfilled, even that the sun isn't shining.

How many times have you 'chased a loss'? You may have gambled £25, lost it and then spent £250 (or far more), determined to win back that original £25. The original stake might even have been a free bonus from the casino, as they know how a gambler's mind works far better than any therapist or counsellor and play on that in order to suck ever more funds from you. Why do we do such a thing? Well, all we are desperate to do is stay in the perceived comfort of the 'twilight zone'. We become irrationally angry and excessively competitive to win back that money even though it costs us huge sums.

I strongly believe that this competitiveness is a character flaw in a compulsive gambler's make-up, one that once recognized can be dealt with in order to overcome our addiction. We may not even recognize the competitiveness in ourselves – it certainly doesn't mean that all compulsive gamblers are brilliant sportspeople or razor-sharp salespersons, far from it – but it is something that is dormant within us all.

'OK, I lost!'

Quite simply, and without over-complicating the issue, we need to sit back and say 'OK, I lost.'

That's good and that's positive. You may lose at many other things in life – perhaps you don't get the job you want, or your dream house, car or partner – and still be able to move on. It is even easier with gambling because by accepting that simple statement 'OK, I lost', you actually begin *winning*. What did I say earlier about all gambling being competitive and challenging you? Well, by not accepting the challenge, you win. The casino, bookmakers, bingo hall, online casino, race track, lottery and so forth challenge you to bet with them in order for them to beat you. Very simply, you beat them by keeping your money in your pocket. They lose the challenge; you win the challenge. You are the winner; they are the loser. (You will notice throughout this book that I hold the gambling industry in no respect at all, and you should adopt the same attitude. Other than perhaps the tobacco industry, I can think of no other industry that takes so much from society and gives back so little, or is so destructive of the family unit.)

Let's assume you have accepted that it is the mood or mindset whereby your troubles and stresses are put on hold that you 'enjoy' while gambling. Where is the harm in that? After all, we all need a bit of time out from modern life. Well, the problem is that as you gamble more, and almost inevitably lose more, the pressures and stresses on you increase. You then need to keep on returning more and more often to the 'twilight zone' to escape them, and the vicious cycle and addiction begins.

This whole methodology is again comparable to being a smoker. Almost all smokers use excuses such as 'Smoking helps me concentrate' or 'Smoking relaxes me' to justify what they themselves (as well as everyone else) know is a disgusting, dangerous, antisocial habit. Such excuses just aren't true. The only reason the smoker believes that smoking relaxes her or helps her concentrate is because she hasn't been relaxed and able to concentrate since the nicotine from her last cigarette left her body (usually after just 15 minutes or so). Only after she lights another cigarette is she replacing that nicotine in her body, thus becoming relaxed and able to concentrate again. She believes that the cigarette has solved her problem rather than causing it. If I were teaching you how to give up smoking rather than gambling, I wouldn't suggest you use nicotine patches or chew nicotine gum as this means your life still revolves around nicotine.

So you have read this far, and I hope I've got you thinking! You may be fighting these ideas because you want to over-complicate things, or perhaps you feel you are different from all the others. You may be trying to protect your gambling at this stage, or justifying to yourself that if it was this easy, you could have stopped a long time ago. Or perhaps you are arguing that it is an addiction and you can never be cured of an addiction because, as I mention above, you have been conditioned to think that way. Well, I'm afraid all that is rubbish. Addictions are habits, and habits can be broken. Don't believe me? Then ask yourself how quickly you break the habit of driving on the left when you go over to France or holiday in America. It is immediate, and if it wasn't you probably wouldn't be alive to read this book! Millions of people have successfully beaten smoking, drinking and drug addictions, and all three of those are addictions whereby we physically alter our bodies and minds via external substances.

Let's put that entire paragraph into a simple little sentence:

'We don't *need* to gamble to *survive!*'

You can write this out ten times if you like (see Chapter 9, 'The futility and danger of gambling', for more on affirmations) to make it sink deep into your subconscious.

What do we care whether we call it an addiction or a habit? Just accept that you can kick it totally and move on. Think of all the other habits, such as nail biting, nose picking or thumb sucking (or a hundred others, I'm sure), that you have already overcome, and convince yourself that gambling is no worse, and more importantly, no more difficult to overcome, than those. You have made an incredible start. Why not reduce your local bookmaker, casino or online gaming site to nothing more than a childish habit and become determined to kick the gambling habit just as easily as you kicked other little habits?

I will show you how to stop digging the hole any deeper, and then show you how to cut each upward step back out of that hole, and back into that place called Life.

Recap

1 Accept that it isn't the action of gambling itself that you are addicted to, it is the 'twilight zone' whereby all your real problems are temporarily ignored while you gamble.

2 Accept that there is nothing physically preventing you from stopping gambling altogether and that your gambling is just a grubby little habit, the same as picking your nose at the age of six; one which you can kick just as easily, with a bit of instruction from me and self-belief from you.

3 Accept that by not dealing with your 'real world' problems while you gambled, you have worsened them rather than improved them.

4 Say out aloud to yourself and anyone else nearby, 'OK, I lost.' That phrase is in the *past* tense.

5 Say out loud to yourself and anyone else nearby, 'I win, gambling loses.' That phrase is in the *present* tense.

6 Rejoice and get excited about the fact that you are stopping gambling altogether and beginning a new life.

7 Promise yourself that you will read the whole of this book.

3

The Release: creating the 'rock bottom'

'If you are really smart, you know when to stop talking and start listening!'

This chapter is intended for both the compulsive gambler and his or her partner (or family or friends). It looks at how the gambler and his support can create a confrontation where the full extent of the gambling is clearly exposed and seen for what it is. I call it 'the Release' because, however painful, it nearly always is a release for gambler and loved ones alike – there has been so much secrecy that it is a huge relief all round to get it out into the open.

In recovery circles, it used to be thought that before an addict could begin to recover, it was necessary to reach 'rock bottom' – a low point beyond which the addict could not sink. These days it's increasingly accepted that this isn't always necessary. Indeed, many counsellors and recovery programmes now encourage the *creation* of a rock bottom. This may sound artificial, but to be honest, if you're reading this book, things are probably bad enough right now, aren't they?

Who to work with

The kind of confrontation referred to above, the 'Release', is usually best created with your partner, family member or close friend.

If you aren't in a relationship or with a steady partner, then you need to find the closest person to you who has been affected by your gambling: possibly a parent, brother or sister, best friend, trusted work colleague or even bank manager. You must have someone you can turn to – but do make sure that person *is* trusted. Just because you feel guilty, it doesn't mean you have to bare your soul and tell all to the first person who comes along.

The 'rock bottom' myth

While many people do hit an all-time personal low that propels them into seeking treatment for their addiction, a 'rock bottom' is not an absolute requirement. In fact, it can be a harmful myth. Ask yourself, how much worse do things need to get? Bearing in mind the grim statistic that the suicide rate for gambling addicts is 20 times higher than that for non-gamblers, waiting to hit rock bottom could mean the difference between life and death. You don't have to wait for life to become unbearable.

Some kinds of therapy now focus on starting the healing process without waiting for the addict to hit 'rock bottom', or on creating a rock bottom, sometimes with the help of family and friends – so-called 'intervention'. A typical intervention usually includes the following steps:

- *Planning*: researching the extent of the problem, maybe with the help of written material such as diaries, and, in the case of gambling, bank statements, betting slips and so on.
- *Forming an intervention team*: either with loved ones or, if unavoidable, alone, who decide on a consistent plan of action and set a date from which things will start changing.
- *Confrontation*: a key step. Either the addict or the loved one arranges a face-to-face meeting in which the full extent of the problem is disclosed.
- *Deciding on consequences* (for family and friends): if your loved one can't or won't change and/or undertake treatment, a decision needs to be made about any action to be taken, such as asking the addict to move out or arranging a separation.

The rest of this chapter looks at how to start being an active participant in your own healing, rather than waiting passively for events to roll you along. Don't wait for rock bottom!

If you really have no one, or prefer to do this alone, you'll have to play devil's advocate yourself. Why not visualize your brain being divided into two, with the left-hand side being the side that wants to quit gambling (the positive side), while the right-hand side doesn't think you can give up (the negative side). Draw a diagram of this if you think it helps, and label both sides with pros and cons.

However you do it, each side will need to keep quiet and listen to the other in order for this to work. The compulsive gambler probably has a huge amount bottled up that he'll want to get out. I'd be very surprised if he isn't hugely relieved that everything is finally out in the open, despite the pain he knows he is going to face. It is enormously important that we capture and use the essence of that relief. It is a purging of the soul, a dam-burst of emotions and an outflowing of all the lies he has told for so many years. If, as his loved one, you continually butt in or fly at him during this outflow (however justified your reaction), the danger is that the compulsive gambler will clam up and the purge will only be a third or half done.

During this talking and listening both sides need to employ a technique called bracketing. This means that if you are the listener, you put mental brackets around your thoughts and emotions and don't let them out until the talker has finished.

Ask yourselves: Do both sides agree to listen to the other side and allow them to speak? If yes, then we can move on. If no, then maybe try to arrange another time to begin this.

Creating your 'rock bottom'

Sam

In the course of my confrontation, or Release, I had a real moment of clarity regarding my arrogance and immaturity around gambling, and it took my 20-year-old stepdaughter to bring it to my attention. My wife and her daughter were looking through ten years of devastation in the form of bank statements when my stepdaughter turned to my wife and said, 'He really was a rubbish gambler, Mum, wasn't he?' They then both burst into fits of laughter. When my wife told me this, I immediately became defensive, blustering and stuttering that I wasn't, it was just that I couldn't keep my winnings, that I won a lot, particularly when I played blackjack – and so on. I then heard myself speaking and recognized what a crock of garbage I was talking, and said to myself, 'Admit it, you were a rubbish gambler!' Then I laughed and felt a huge weight lift from my shoulders.

'If you don't know why you failed, you are no wiser than when you began'

Having been a compulsive gambler myself, I know how many times you may have had a devastating loss, be it on the horses, internet casino, land-based casino or online bingo, and said to yourself 'That's it, I must stop!' You have been convinced that you have to stop because you know how much money you have just lost. You have a good overall idea how much money you have lost since you started gambling, and you know only too well how much pain and damage the gambling is doing to yourself and those you love. If you are anything like me, then after you've told yourself that you must stop, you feel a brief tingle of relief, because you actually think you will stop. You think it can't be that difficult to stop, even if this is the fifteenth or fiftieth time you've tried. Each time you try to stop you are more convinced you can stop because you've lost even more money, so it is even more important that you do stop. Well, how is this time going to be any different? I'll tell you.

Each previous time you tried stopping, you maybe thought that you had hit 'rock bottom'. The fact of the matter is that you didn't hit your rock bottom. The gambling made you hit *a* rock bottom which you thought must be *the* rock bottom.

Think of yourself sinking in the cloudy mire of gambling but never reaching the sea bed. The floor of this mire actually consists of a series of layers, and all that happens after you have hit one floor is that the gambling will continue to roll you along until you fall off that floor, down to the lower level below. Unless you initiate something drastic, it is the gambling that is creating your rock bottom each time (usually after another catastrophic loss), not you. You cannot begin to pick yourself up, either physically or metaphorically, until you have reached the very lowest level, the actual bottom.

What we do with our system, starting with the Release, is to take you from whichever level you are on and throw you straight down to the very bottom, so that you can immediately start climbing back up again. If either you, or more probably your partner, initiate the rock bottom – either by you confessing fully to your gambling or your partner confronting you – then you are the ones in control, not the gambling.

Reaching that point, so that you can really begin your recovery, takes some courage, and as gamblers we don't usually do courage very well! We don't enjoy confrontation and prefer to slip under the covers of our addiction and into our dream world, in which we finally get the big win and life is rosy.

Now I want to lead you through the process to that rock bottom, and the beginning of recovery. There will be a step-by-step recap at the end of the chapter, but it is important to read and fully understand each step, rather than try and rush through it.

Step 1: Preparing for the confrontation or confession

If you have decided, either as a compulsive gambler or the partner or friend of a compulsive gambler, to commit to giving up gambling, or to confronting your gambling partner, then this is where we begin.

If you are the gambler, then I would urge you to start *now*, literally *now*. Don't commit to doing this after your next big loss, or in a week's time, or at the beginning of next month, or if the bets you've already laid today or this week don't win. Do it *now*. If you are following this book, you will already have admitted to yourself the scale of your problem and accepted that nothing is going to change unless you initiate that change.

In order to look at this in a cold, clear light with an uncluttered head, it is strongly suggested that you take yourself away completely from your usual environment. There are a huge number of inexpensive options (see our website <www.gamblersaloud.com> for some ideas). One effective idea is to go abroad, even if it is just across to France or Europe for a couple of days. The aim is to disrupt your normal patterns of behaviour, and to put barriers in the way of your gambling. Most probably, it will be much less easy to walk into a foreign bookmaker's and place a bet, and you will be less comfortable walking into a foreign casino or on to a foreign race track. That just leaves the internet to overcome. It will help if you choose a more remote location where the internet isn't so easily available, but you have to make a commitment not to go and search out an internet café and begin gambling online again.

If going abroad is not possible, do your best to get away from your usual haunts for a while.

Tools to take

Before you go, do some packing. Obviously, you're not going to take huge wads of cash or a wallet full of credit cards, though lack of such facilities never stopped the really determined gambler. Do take:

- this book;
- a CD with your favourite music (see pages 42–3 for information about how music may help);
- a notebook in which to jot down any thoughts.

Have a look at the suggestions for downloading on my website (see Useful addresses). Before you leave, download the spoken part – which gives you a summary of each chapter of the book – and the music suggestions. Even better, make your own on another CD or your MP3, interspersing your own music (if you don't like my choices) with the key points.

While you are away, try physically as well as mentally to detach yourself from your gambling and your past. Sit down and read this book attentively. When you have done that, read it again. Think, think and think again about what your gambling has done to you, is doing to you, and will do to you. At the very least, give yourself a *chance*. You still deserve this one last chance of putting yourself right again. Don't go looking for others or calling others to get their opinion on this. Did you ever pick up the phone to a friend, or ask someone at the pub, 'What do you think? Shall I become a compulsive gambler?' So why go looking for anyone else to decide you should get out of the addiction? Only you can solve this and commit to treating yourself at this point. It is why you have to get away.

If you are the friend or partner of a compulsive gambler and you are wondering whether to confront him or not, getting away completely for a few days should be equally effective in helping you decide. This decision can't be made for you. I have tried, within these pages, to give you an idea of the emotions you may go through, but every individual and every relationship is different, so again, only you can decide your way forward. The aim is to generate some understanding of what it is that has afflicted your partner. Find a quiet sanctuary for a couple of days, in which to make that momentous decision whether to confront him or not.

It does take courage – from the gambler, too, of course. Some gamblers are definitely screaming out to be caught. Even if they can't bring themselves to sit their partner down and confess all, they may employ fairly obvious sign language – leaving betting slips in their wallet and bookies' pens in their pockets, leaving bank or credit card statements on the table or mantelpiece, and so on. However, if a partner doesn't pick up the clues, then you will have to initiate the confession. Bear in mind as well, if you do leave clues around, that they may also be spotted by a sharp-eyed child.

If you are a non-gambler or the partner of a gambler, you may well find it bizarre that I'm advising compulsive gamblers how to get caught, but sometimes this is what is needed to make the start. At this point we love you, we hate ourselves, we do actually hate our gambling and we are asking for help. We know you are going to get angry, and we know so well that you fully deserve to, but if you can confront us with our gambling, then everyone can move forward, on whichever route that takes us.

Step 2: The confrontation – the whole truth and nothing but ...

'If you tell the truth you don't have to remember anything.'

Mark Twain

If you are anything like me, then this is the moment you have been waiting for, for quite a long time. However, don't for one minute think that makes it easy. Despite your desire to tell all, and the relief of it being out in the open, you may still find yourself being defensive, even petulant.

The gambler has been 'in control' all the time she has been 'out of control'. That is, it was she who was throwing finances away and running the family into the ground, and however unlikely it sounds, it's not something that can easily be given up. She managed – or mismanaged – her life, it was she who staged it all, and stepping down and admitting failure can feel like the end of the world. Letting others in on this can be even more frightening. The invasion of a private or secret world can create feelings of vulnerability even when that invasion is both invited and needed. In addition, guilt may threaten to smother you as it all comes out.

Don't be surprised if you break down in tears, no matter what size or sex you are. This is the dam bursting, the release of everything that has been held back by you for so long. So let it come, though it probably won't all happen in one go. And, of course, not everyone expresses remorse in tears.

However you do express it, though, it is vitally important that you really do get everything out. Don't go for half measures, for whatever reason, for example if you think you can't hurt your partner so much by telling him everything. It really is all or nothing at this point. I tried hiding one gold credit card that I'd run up gambling debts on rather than confess to that as well – a bit like an alcoholic keeping back just one bottle when all the others have been ostentatiously thrown out. Bear in mind that secrecy is an addict's need, and that secrecy and privacy can be conflated. Secrecy has more to do with being selfish, dishonest and immature; find other ways to be private, such as going for a quiet walk.

Step 3: Write your gambling history

While it's natural to confide first in the person or people closest to you, it's also essential to broaden the outflow of information to everyone affected by your gambling, such as parents, brothers, in-laws and friends whom you have borrowed from. This is not only important for you, but vital for your non-gambling partner, who needs help and support every bit as much as you do.

One way to do this is to write a potted history of your gambling from the earliest memories, maybe starting with the most recent and working backwards. This can be done as a story, or as a time-line – whatever you find most natural. Another helpful format is the CV, adding your gambling history instead of your career history to the key dates (see example in appendix). This is an easy and effective way of doing it, given that most people have a CV of some sort. Basically what I did was rehash my CV, including the salaries I had earned at each job, along with any significant outgoings, and detail my gambling activity and its intensity alongside those various jobs. Such a system allows people to see that maybe you didn't gamble more or less when you were in better- or worse-paid jobs. You will see in Chapter 6 that this is the first of the gambler's 'signposts'.

This gambling history is extremely helpful, indeed, vital. It helps purge the gambler of what he has done, and allows him to be honest in black and white; it also allows all those around to begin to understand the extent of the gambling problem. At this point, family and friends need to know that this isn't a little problem whereby the gambler put £10 too much on the Grand National or blew £50 at her last visit to Blackpool! It is essential for everyone's sakes that it is done, and done quickly.

Harry

After my gambling history became public and the floodgates opened on my past, I was being everything that I hadn't been since gambling took over my life – emotional, honest, forthright, brave, attentive, focused and passionate. By the time the shock of that wore off a little (around three to four days) I was so far into it, and so committed to stopping gambling, that there was no turning back, even if I'd considered it. That is what you need. It is a lot harder telling those you love and who love you as opposed to a group of strangers in a room or in an online forum, and so it commits you to succeeding to a far greater degree. Strike while the iron is hot and get it all out. That is what turns your character around, and from there we can build you up again, to a stronger and better human being.

Something you may feel in these early days, when everything is coming out, is just an inkling of pride, in that finally after so many years of lies and deceit, you are actually beginning to be honest, both to your-self and those around you. Maybe I was clutching at straws, given the devastation that I'd caused everyone, but if you don't grab hold of such feelings and exploit them, then you will bury yourself under a deluge of self-hatred, low self-esteem and guilt.

You will see in Chapter 5 that accepting that your addiction was an illness, along with these little rays of honesty, can be the start of building up a new life; so it is vitally important at this stage not to beat yourself mentally to a pulp.

'Team CG'

Another great reason for 'spreading the message' about your release from gambling is that it is the opposite of what you would probably normally do. So many of us, when we hit a crisis, go into lockdown mode. We want to handle it ourselves and not burden others. We may feel this either through shame about our past actions or out of compassion for those whom we would like to tell; we think 'They have their own problems, I can't give them mine.' If you try to deal with such a major issue as stopping gambling on your own, you place a massive burden on yourself while trying to cope in isolation. Additionally, you are not changing your pattern and routine (see Chapter 2) because most probably you will have tried on your own to stop gambling countless times before. By involving everyone else this time, you are disrupting your habit in a major way, and therefore breaking it.

By involving as many others as you can, you are building a team around you, and in broad terms, teams are usually much more effective at solving problems than individuals. The benefits of having such a network don't just extend to the compulsive gambler, of course. Partners need strength, advice, guidance and a sense of proportion, all of which can be derived from 'Team CG'. Parents and family members, friends and even co-workers all need similar support in order to help both themselves and the gambler through this crisis.

If you are the partner, friend or relative of the compulsive gambler, you are certainly going to need help and support – even if it's just someone other than the gambler to talk to. Don't try to be a hero and take all this on your shoulders. It's understandable you may feel devastated that someone you loved and trusted has effectively been lying to you all this time, and you may well need to discuss that with others close to you, as well as with the gambler. If, for whatever reason (perhaps shame, embarrassment or fear of causing pain), you try to keep this between the two of you, it's much more likely that the recovery will collapse. You, as the partner or friend, risk being overwhelmed by the pain and magnitude of it all, and the compulsive gambler by the guilt and shame. With the burden shared more widely, both of you can draw strength from others. In purely practical terms, involving everyone affected by the compulsive gambler ensures that all future 'easy' sources of money will immediately dry up, so even if the gambler is tempted to return to gambling, money will be far less forthcoming than before.

Step 4: Say goodbye to your lover (gambling)

In fact, no, don't! Slam the door in her face and get her out of your life for ever! Seeing your gambling as a lover is a concept my wife came up with at the very beginning of my recovery, and has been very important for both of us. We believe it is a new idea, and, as with everything contained in our system, we want to pass it on. It has helped her focus on 'the gambling' and treat it as though I have been having a 20-year affair, which in effect is the truth. As is common for partners discovering such a fact, trust and honesty fly straight out of the window, but it has helped her to rationalize and understand the problem a little better.

During the last years of my addiction, particularly while we were overseas, my wife was actually convinced that I was carrying on a physical affair. She has told me of smelling my clothes, checking my BlackBerry for calls made or received, and discussing it with friends. On reflection, the signs of my obsession with gambling must have been very similar to those of an actual affair. Let's look at a few of the character traits that the gambler may develop while gambling:

- severe mood swings, from very happy to down and withdrawn;
- unexplained or poorly explained absences, or taking longer over simple tasks outside the house, like shopping or buying a newspaper;
- inability to relax and enjoy each other's company;
- eagerness to leave the house alone at any opportunity;
- spontaneous gifts (for which read apologies) or flowers;
- continual phone calls to one's partner throughout the day, but particularly at lunch time, in order to 'clear the coast' and lessen the likelihood of him or her calling while the gambler is in the bookie's;
- unusually late returns from company nights out;
- resentment at spending time or money on friends for entertainment;
- total secrecy regarding credit card or bank statements;
- extended use of the computer while on leave or at weekends, supposedly for work purposes.

None of the above traits are specific either to gambling or having an affair, but I'm sure if you asked someone who has just discovered that their partner has been cheating on them for 20 years with an actual lover, nearly all those would come up.

Harry
The key issue that made it even easier for my wife to relate to gambling as my lover, was that as a VIP Gold Member of my internet casino I was actually provided with an account manageress, Eva, to attend to my every wish and enhance my gambling experience. She was like a seductive, glossy escort used to suck me dry of every cent I possessed. I got lots of bonuses, offers of trips to Paris and Ascot – you name it. I even sent my wife a hamper of cheap chocolates, champagne and body products on her birthday, without letting it be known it was from the casino. My gambling was our little secret, and Eva used to write me chatty little notes to see how I was doing and to stroke my ego, just as an escort tells a client how great he is in bed, how he is the special one for her and not like all the others.

One advantage of viewing your gambling as a lover is that you can imagine that the affair has come to an end. Why not write a 'Dear John' letter in which you tell the casino, online site, dog track or other gambling venue that you no longer care for it. Imagine that you are in the position of a lover who wishes to make his or her feelings crystal clear and leave no room for confusion, no possibility that the relationship could in any way, shape or form resume in the future.

I'm not suggesting that you actually post the letter. Its power is in helping you to phrase a final and unequivocal message: you and I are over for good!

Self-exclusion

Some gambling venues operate a voluntary self-exclusion programme, whereby you sign an agreement not to enter or use the gambling areas on pain of expulsion.

If internet sites such as casinos, gambling or bingo were your major problem then I suggest you sit down, on your own or with your partner or other supporter, and write to all those that you have an account with. Tell them that you are a compulsive or addicted gambler and that you are closing your account permanently and never want to hear from them again in any form (see example in appendix). They'll probably write back saying how sorry they are, how they promote 'responsible gambling', how most of their loyal customers enjoy gambling in their own homes – but do not expect them to send a cheque for next month's mortgage! They are done with you. Their time is money so they are already off on to the next poor soul. You meant nothing to them other than money while you were throwing it at them and you mean nothing to them now you are dried up.

If land-based casinos, slot machines, bingo or betting shops were your problem, I would strongly advise you and your partner or other support person to go round every single one you used in your vicinity and together ban yourself. This is part of the process of confirming to yourself and your partner that you really are serious this time. It will be embarrassing, for sure, and you'll probably feel like a naughty schoolchild, but that discomfort can be very valuable. The louder and more pronounced you make the process the better. Do it in front of as many other punters as you can. You need pain and embarrassment at this point and your partner or friend will find it helps to see and feel your pain.

Step 5: Breaking up your behaviour pattern and routines

You have now broken your routine of gambling and thinking about gambling. You have caused yourself a lot of pain by finally being honest about your gambling, either to yourself or to the people closest to you. We now need to keep you on this bandwagon. Banning yourself from land-based or internet sites is good, as is a computer block to stop you accessing those sites, but these are short-term 'barriers', all of which can be got around. We need to look at the long term.

Exercise

One of the greatest activities you can take up, and one of the strongest barriers to going back to gambling, is exercise. It has been scientifically proven that regular exercise makes us feel better, irrespective of whether or not we have gambling problems. While caught up in compulsive gambling, you probably will not have been looking after your body. You will most likely not have been exercising at all and you won't have cared about your nutrition. Additionally, it's likely that you'll have been placing your body under tremendous mental and physical stress because of your gambling and the problems associated with it. In order to combat that, you need to replace the negative habit of gambling with the positive habit of regular exercise. It is that simple.

Some of you may be thinking, 'That's fine for you to say, but how can I afford gym membership when I'm this much in debt?' Who mentioned anything about a gym? Get out and walk; it's free! Walk to work, walk early in the morning, walk late in the evening, walk alone, walk with someone else, walk at weekends, but walk. If you want to go further, find the cash for a second-hand bike and start cycling everywhere.

The point is to stop finding reasons and excuses not to exercise and get out there and do it! If, like me, you always found reasons *not* to stop gambling, why not kick the habit of finding reasons not to do things and get into the habit of finding reasons *to* do things. Once you begin regular exercise, you will begin feeling better about your body, which will make you feel better about your mind. You will *need* the regular exercise. You will *not* need the gambling. Once again:

You win, they lose.

Other ways to break up your routine

Some gamblers spend 10 to 20 hours a week gambling, so there can be quite a gap to fill once you stop. The following are things you can do to usefully occupy your time:

- Call a friend you haven't spoken to for some time. Reconnecting is an important part of recovery.
- Spend time with positive, loving people.
- Polish all your shoes.
- Go out and buy yourself some new clothes – if you're broke, as you may well be, some charity shops have nearly-new bargains.
- Go to a Gamblers Anonymous meeting.
- Brainstorm with a friend or partner to see if you can think of a new business that could make you some money in ways unconnected with gambling.
- Volunteer some time to a charity.
- Take a short holiday or even a day away.
- Go to a museum, art gallery or concert; some lunchtime concerts are free.

- Start a new hobby or pick up an old one – gardening, painting, writing.
- Enrol for a course in a language or some other form of study.

Recap

1 Take yourself and your partner away from your normal environment, perhaps abroad, in order to remove the immediate temptation to gamble.
2 Agree between yourselves to listen calmly to each other, so that *everything* comes out from the compulsive gambler and the partner or friend.
3 If you are the compulsive gambler, confess to the person who means the most to you or who has been the most affected by your gambling. Confess to absolutely every part of your gambling and give as accurate an estimation as you can of the amount you have gambled in the past week, month and year(s). If you really have nobody in your life to confess to, then, finally, be honest with yourself and address your gambling.
4 If you are the partner or friend, confront the gambler *today*!
5 Write a brief but complete gambling 'history' of when and where you have gambled, ever since you started, and send it to every member of your family and every friend affected by your gambling. Follow that up with phone calls to discuss it further with them.
6 Accept that you can't do this alone and form 'Team CG', the group of family and friends who will help you through this process and whose help you will need to recover from your gambling.
7 Cancel membership of all internet casinos or gambling sites and exclude yourself from every location you gambled in. It may be embarrassing and humiliating, but aim to do this in the company of your partner or friend.
8 Take up exercise or other activities, such as volunteering for a charity or simply getting back in touch with friends, in order to fill the time previously occupied by gambling.

Despite the shock of this process to all involved, this has been a big step forward for everyone, and you are ready to move on to the next chapter.

4

Gamblers Aloud

This chapter explains in more detail our unique approach to stopping gambling. You will have seen in previous chapters that I'm not just regurgitating what is already out there, and in some cases I am actually suggesting the opposite of 'conventional' wisdom. Why? Because I am convinced that compulsive gambling can be kicked by every single individual if he or she has the commitment. I call that approach 'Gamblers Aloud'.

This chapter is placed here, rather than at the beginning of the book, because you, the compulsive gambler, and your loved ones, probably wanted action from the moment you picked the book up. I hope that by now any compulsive gamblers reading it have broken the routine of gambling and caused themselves sufficient pain to really commit to curing themselves. Now we begin to look at the longer term and the months and years ahead, and how you can remain gambling free for the rest of your lives.

Gamblers Aloud says two things:

Gamblers, it's good to shout it out 'aloud' and not be anonymous.
Gamblers are 'allowed'.

Maybe you think I am just trying to come up with a catchy 'soundbite', playing on the word 'aloud/allowed', but it encapsulates what I am about and how I am offering you a very different approach from anything that is out there. So please don't discount it.

Why say it aloud?

Twelve-step programmes with a focus on anonymity – such as Gamblers Anonymous, Alcoholics Anonymous (AA) and Narcotics Anonymous (NA) – have all made important achievements since AA was started by Bill Wilson in 1935, especially in times and places where alcoholics and drug and other addicts have had to cope with social stigma. Anonymity in these groups acts as a reminder to place (in the words of AA) 'principles before personalities'. Anonymity may provide valuable privacy, especially for new members, who might feel too ashamed and vulnerable to attend otherwise, and helps protect the group from exploitation, particularly at the level of the media.

However, think for a moment of some of the many other causes or movements in the last 50 years: gay rights, Aids awareness, anti-fur campaigns, animal rights, hunting; or, going even further back, the suffragettes and votes for women. The list is endless and hugely diverse, but all these movements have one thing in common. Their participants weren't anonymous. They stood up and told the world what they wanted to achieve, and in virtually all cases they achieved their aim or at the very least made their individual cause better known.

Yes, I can hear you saying, but I don't want to start an anti-gambling campaign. I just want to stop myself gambling! I understand and I'm not proposing a movement like that. The point is the power of *not* being anonymous when you are coming out of your gambling coma. I wasn't – indeed, telling people about what I'd done and how low I'd got while gambling was a cornerstone of my success.

Gambling in itself involves a kind of anonymity that, to me, is part of its destructive power. What have we compulsive gamblers done for the last two, or 20, years, or however long you have been in its grip? We've gone around lying about our finances, where we've been, where we are going, why we have money, why we don't have money, and we've lied about our emotions. We've been outwardly happy when inwardly we are crushed by another loss, or we've inwardly wanted to dance with joy after a big win but outwardly had to disguise it with emotional neutrality, so that we don't give the game away and can keep our ill-gotten gains to throw away at a later date. My problem, when I was confronted with my compulsive gambling, was how could 'anonymity' ever be a cure or help me come out of what was clearly an 'anonymous' problem?

Maybe being open is the last thing you want to do. Maybe you feel too ashamed of your gambling to let those closest to you know how bad it really was. That's natural, but telling them, and then detailing in writing your gambling history and giving them your account, as I outlined in Chapter 3, will allow them to start trusting you. And that may lead to a measure of respect. Trust me, when you seemingly have nothing, a small measure of trust and respect from a loved one seems like the jackpot!

Don't just look at what you get out of telling everyone. Consider as well what others will get out of knowing what was wrong with you. That is the beginning of humility, which we'll deal with in Chapter 10 and is key to your recovery. Of course, not everyone will simply accept it and move on. It could even cost you your marriage and/or job, but if you don't kick your compulsive gambling then you are likely to lose those anyway. So, for once, you literally can't lose.

Why not GA?

While more research is needed to establish a clear picture of their effectiveness, anonymous self-help groups such as Gamblers Anonymous have attracted various criticisms. Among those levelled at GA itself are, crucially, low levels of success – one study indicated that just 8 per cent of those attending remained totally abstinent after one year, and it is generally believed to be more successful for those with severe problems. Some researchers have also suggested that women may be alienated by what is sometimes said to be its macho or overtly 'male' culture, for example what is claimed to be a confrontational approach and an emphasis on practical issues such as employment and financial concerns, at the expense of spiritual and interpersonal issues. All in all, GA is often perceived as helpful, but not enough, and as something that works best in conjunction with other forms of help, such as therapy or other support groups such as NA or AA.

You don't necessarily always need sympathy and kind words from fellow compulsive gamblers, or a weekly shot of hearing other people's problems. While some may find initial comfort in going to meetings and seeing and hearing that other people have the same or worse problems than you, how often do you need to hear that? While it may help to know that 'there are others out there', some gamblers feel that the 'rooms' (as the anonymous meetings are called) provide artificial security, and that they derive more benefit from working much closer to home – that is, taking responsibility themselves for kicking the habit, making amends to those affected by the gambling, reintegrating themselves into society, and going on to lead a meaningful life that benefits others.

Harry
Time spent explaining your compulsive gambling to other compulsive gamblers is time not spent explaining to those affected by your gambling. They are the people that should matter in your life. What are you looking for in those meetings? Perhaps a 'confessional' approach. 'Sorry I succumbed to the temptation of Leaden Express in the 2.45 at Newmarket this afternoon but it was my first relapse in two weeks!' Tea, sympathy and biscuits don't help much in that situation, or not for me.

There is also the danger that you may hear discouraging news at a meeting which may have a negative effect on you. I do not wish to deny that for many people these kinds of meeting are helpful, just to point out that they are not a panacea and they may not suit everyone.

Alternatives to gambling

Many people gamble because they do not know what else to do. It's helpful therefore to find an alternative recreational activity or hobby. We are all creatures of habit and tend to go to certain places at certain times, where we do certain things. Gambling can be habitual in this way, so having an alternative activity, something engrossing and enjoyable, is a good idea. I can't tell you what it will be but I can suggest that, unless it's illegal or harmful to your health, it's bound to be better for you than gambling. As I write elsewhere, I recommend exercise as a great alternative to gambling.

Once I'd stopped gambling, I was often questioned as to how I now spent my time or occupied my mind. Well, quite frankly, I got on and lived. I don't think most normal people spend a huge amount of time wondering what they will do all day! The ex-gambler, or the person trying to stop gambling, should have far less time on her hands than normal people, as she should be desperate to make up for all the wasted hours, days or weeks spent gambling! Whether or not you choose to go to a support group, the ultimate aim is fundamentally to change your outlook on life, now it is gambling free, and I sincerely hope this book will help towards that.

The power of music

Music has the power to lift us up, drop us down, make us romantic, reflective, aggressive or calm, so how can it possibly not help us to overcome our compulsive gambling? We anchor ourselves to certain songs; 'our tune', for example, a piece of music associated with a special moment you shared with someone very close to you and which sends a shiver down your spine and stops you dead in your tracks whenever you hear it, even ten years later.

The aim is to take the power of music and drip feed yourself 'positivity', whereby you have to try harder to be down than up, or negative rather than positive, while listening to it.

- Make a CD or MP3 collection of your favourite music. Spend some time on this. Go back to your favourites from before the gambling days; choose music associated with high points and good times in your life.
- Choose some music together with your partner or family that means something to you all; special moments, holidays, successes. Listen to it together.
- Investigate the Gamblers Aloud music download (see Useful addresses). It isn't full of mating whales' calls, Peruvian panpipes, waterfalls or the call of a skylark across a lush green meadow on a crisp spring English morning! Why not listen to the download while reading the book, particularly when you are away from your home? I have put on it key, bulleted points of the system and interspersed them with tracks that to me are relevant. If you're making your own CD or MP3 collection, you might find it helpful to follow this format and key in a similar narrative – whatever works for you!

The aim is to assault the gambler's senses from as many different angles as possible, in the same way that casinos, bingo halls, bookies and particularly online casinos do. Ever wondered why fruit machines ring bells when someone wins, or why bookies and casinos are so brightly lit? Why there are no clocks in casinos and exits are so hard to find? They are attacking your senses, confusing you while still offering you the apparently safe haven of the casino floor. Physically they make it difficult for you to leave because they know mentally you are also having difficulty leaving. Well, we're fighting fire with fire. You are reading this book, and you are hearing this system through music; and in another chapter you'll also see how we use tactile objects to help (see Chapter 8, 'The chip of change').

Gamblers 'Allowed' – getting it in perspective

The other aspect of Gamblers Aloud is the Gamblers 'Allowed' message. What do I mean by that? I mean that it is OK that you were a gambler. I'm not for a minute proposing you should ever be proud of it. Pride should be saved for when you have kicked it, through following this system. Why though do I say it is OK that you were a gambler? Because we all have baggage! Some of us (by 'us' I mean 'normal' people) are overweight, underweight, anorexic or bulimic, alcoholics, drug addicts, nicotine addicts with very serious problems; others may be lazy or underachieve, work too hard and don't see enough of their family; yet others are unfaithful to their partners, or even shop too much. The point I'm making is that none of us, or at best very few of us, are perfect and most of us have significant faults. Is the father who can't (or doesn't) control his weight and dies of a heart attack at 45 leaving a wife and two young children any less cruel than the compulsive gambler who never has enough money or time to spend on his family? It's impossible to say, of course, but please don't feel you have to ostracize or alienate yourself because you were a compulsive gambler.

Recap

1 Accept that an anonymous cure to an anonymous problem isn't going to work and that you need to tell those closest to you, and those affected by your gambling, about it.

2 Resolve firmly *not* to take the easy option of telling only strangers and fellow sufferers about your problem, and to take instead the much harder option of telling those closest to you the depth and scale of your problem.

3 Make sure you find alternative activities that will occupy the time you used to spend gambling.

4 Recognize the power of music as a means of healing as well as the need to constantly reinforce the message of this book. Take our CD with you, or make your own version on your MP3 or another CD.

5 Understand that you can't continually 'beat yourself up' about your gambling while hoping to move forward in your life, and recognize that everyone has baggage. Yours was gambling.

Part Two
STAYING STOPPED

5

The illness

What needs to be done now that the compulsive gambling is out in the open, is to pick up the pieces and begin the rebuilding process. You need to deal with yourself, just now. You'll be feeling drained by the last few days and everything that has come out of you, and you'll probably be feeling a little bit scared about where we go from here. That's OK. This book is with you every step of the way.

There is a long-running debate within health circles as to whether a gambling addiction or compulsive gambling can be medically diagnosed and classified as an illness. Furthermore, there are also many questions as to whether drugs can assist in either stopping or controlling people's gambling.

The British Medical Association (BMA) has voiced concerns about problem gambling. Its report 'Gambling addiction and its treatment within the NHS', published in January 2007, called for gambling to be recognized as an addiction that requires treatment on the NHS, where treatment facilities are at best patchy. The BMA has also called on the gambling industry to raise its collective contributions to treatment programmes from £3.6 million in 2007 to at least £10 million.

Such treatment programmes as there are, for example at the ground-breaking Soho Problem Gambling Clinic in London, often use cognitive behavioural therapy (CBT) aimed at helping gamblers change their habits of thinking and behaviour, and create new and more positive ways to live. The Soho Clinic specializes in treating people with co-existing mental health problems, such as bipolar disorder, depression and anxiety, and you may find it easier to access treatment for one of these than for gambling itself. While the BMA's hard-hitting report aimed to increase awareness of problem gambling among the medical profession as well as the general

Gambling and the brain

Several innovative studies have suggested that gambling may involve changes in brain activity, though more research is needed.

For example, one study at Yale University found that problem gamblers experienced unique brain activity changes, with less activity in the areas involved in controlling impulse, when they viewed videos about betting on cards or rolling dice at a casino. The men were scanned with functional magnetic resonance imaging (fMRI), which showed changes in the frontal, paralimbic and limbic brain structures.

Another finding is that gambling has a drug-like effect on the brain. Researchers at Massachusetts General Hospital found that the areas of the brain that respond to winning and losing while gambling appear to be the same as those that respond to cocaine and morphine.

Yet another study at the University of Michigan showed that gamblers' ability to make decisions is affected by losing, which in effect often sets them up for further losses. Choices made after losses were riskier, and were associated with greater loss-related activity than choices made after gains, the study said.

public, GPs still tend to be under-informed about the problem, as well as having limited sources of referral.

Research into compulsive gambling today is still in its early stages and there is no conclusive evidence as to its status as an illness. So it may be most helpful to consider the gambling 'illness' as a useful concept that can be turned to our advantage in recovery. Some people don't need external proof or research to convince themselves that they are ill, and this can be extremely helpful in allowing them to move forward. It can also make things easier to deal with for partners and family.

However, if you're still dubious, let's look at it another way.

Accepting gambling as an illness

Can you convince yourself that you have been affected by gambling in ways that most people aren't? I'm sure you have friends or family who are controlled gamblers, who enjoy just the occasional punt or visit to the races or night out at the casino. You aren't like them, so what is wrong with saying that gambling affects you in a different way to them, as clearly it did? If something affects you in a certain way, and in such a significant and devastating way as gambling did, what is wrong with saying that it 'made you ill'?

Let's try it another way, step by step.

1 You and a friend walk into a field full of spring flowers bulging with pollen.
2 Your friend's eyes start streaming, he or she begins sneezing constantly, and has trouble breathing. You on the other hand have none of those symptoms and are thoroughly enjoying the experience.
3 The reason your friend is suffering so much is that he or she has an *illness* called hay fever.
4 Your friend must then try to avoid all fields of spring flowers, areas of newly cut grass and so forth in order to avoid hay fever.

Then we turn the scenario around to the compulsive gambler.

1 You and your friend the hay fever sufferer go for a night out in the casino.
2 You play roulette, betting £5 chips each time, and then move on to a blackjack table with a £25 minimum stake. You quickly lose the £300 you came in with and draw out another £500 on your credit card in order to try and recoup that first £300. You lose that £500 also. Your friend meantime has played a few slot machines, some £1 minimum blackjack and some 50p minimum roulette. He has had fun watching people and has increased the original £25 he went in with to £34, which he is very happy with. You leave together; his £9 winnings will pay for the kebabs and bus home, while you are devastated by your £800 loss.
3 The reason you are suffering so much is that you have an *illness* called compulsive gambling. You must then try to avoid all casinos, betting offices, race tracks and so forth in order to avoid suffering from compulsive gambling again.

The illness – some 'symptoms'

If you still need convincing, we can compare many of the practical effects of gambling to the symptoms of illness, in the following way:

- Compulsive gambling 'cripples' you, preventing you from doing 'normal' activities like taking your kids to the cinema or out for a pizza, or taking your partner for a relaxed dinner out or even a weekend away.
- It 'disables' you from planning your future, budgeting your finances, advancing or even maintaining your relationships with those close to you and friends, work colleagues, etc.
- The devastating effect that gambling has on you, and all those around you, more often than not 'sickens' you to your core.

Illness and guilt – taking responsibility

The tricky part for the gambler is the balance between brushing off gambling as an illness that couldn't be helped, and dealing with remorse for the pain caused to his or her loved ones. The vast majority of those who start gambling never realize that they are any different from others; they get deeper and deeper into it only to realize afterwards that at some point the gambling has taken over and has become an addiction or illness. With hindsight, gamblers naturally wish they had had the strength of character to stop before it became an addiction, and for that may continually blame themselves. However, it is possible to take responsibility for your behaviour now. Forgive yourself for the past and move on.

By convincing yourself that you have had an illness that can be cured, you allow yourself hope, which right now is a very precious commodity to you. In addition, viewing gambling as an illness does help some of the negative emotions you may be feeling. Gambling addiction feeds on those negative emotions, offering an apparent escape: 'I am your only way out. Gamble again and I might give you that big win that will allow you to climb out of this financial, emotional and moral abyss which you are in now.' The problem is, it won't. It will only dig that pit deeper. By holding on to the idea that you had an illness, you restore a measure of pride within yourself. You will probably be besieged by disbelievers, both compulsive gamblers and non-gamblers, who think it isn't an illness, and perhaps by those that don't consider it as even an addiction. But it doesn't matter so long as you yourself find the concept useful.

In the last analysis, it doesn't matter why you took up gambling. The chances are that they aren't going to find a wonder drug to cure it, just as they haven't for drug addiction, obesity, smoking or drinking, so it is down to you. Allow yourself to see that your mind got you into gambling, and your mind can lead you out of it. One person's problem is another person's challenge. This is your challenge. That's exciting, not frightening.

As the partner or friend of a compulsive gambler, is it so hard to believe that what your partner has had was an illness? Had he always been as he was while in the grip of this addiction? I don't think so, otherwise you would never have been drawn to him in the first place. Compulsive gamblers aren't trying to absolve themselves of blame by recognizing it as an illness.

We don't understand what happened to turn us into the monster we became while in the grip of compulsive gambling. We weren't enjoying ourselves during all this and we could see the pain we were causing you and everyone else, but we literally couldn't stop. If we could have stopped, don't you think we would have stopped?

All we ask, from both the compulsive gambler and the partner or friend, is that you accept that it was an illness, at least enough for us to move on. If you still struggle with that, then just think: if accepting the statement that gambling was an illness is enough to ensure that you (or your compulsive gambling partner) will never gamble again, then surely it is a very small price to pay?

Emotional solitary confinement

This is the state of mind we identified ourselves as being in while gripped by the gambling addiction, and most particularly, while actually gambling. It is the state of mind we called the 'twilight zone' in Chapter 2. We shut everything and everyone else out and concentrate solely on ourselves. We become detached from time and, in many ways, from reality. How many times have you come out of a long, non-stop gambling session, and wondered, literally, where you had been, how you could have blown so much money?

Prolonged compulsive gambling may lead from emotional solitary confinement into a long-term state which I describe as a *state of neutral emotion.*

By a state of neutral emotion, I mean that as compulsive gamblers with an ever-deepening habit, we guard against showing our emotions, which in turn leads us to dilute or restrict our feelings. How often have you had to hide your happiness after a big win, or your sadness after a massive loss? Displaying your emotions openly would have meant giving away the extent of your gambling, and thereby threatening your freedom to continue. So, by having to suppress your emotions constantly, you are in turn deepening your gambling addiction further – usually just when you're getting less and less pleasure from it.

Once you begin to fall into a state of neutral emotion, you are entering a very dangerous stage. You risk making yourself an outcast and becoming very introverted. Even if your partner notices these changes in you (and most inevitably do), it is impossible for him or her to break in or indeed for you to break out. This is where some people find meetings or forums useful, in that they allow people to 'break out' within the confines of anonymity. However, breaking out is not itself a cure, and can offer a false sense of security and hope if you don't go on to take responsibility for your actions and debts, and take active steps to change your ways.

Using emotional solitary confinement

The good news is that we can use our ability to shut everything and everyone else out, to cure ourselves. Go back into the zone of concentration you attain when in front of a slot machine, a roulette wheel, a dog or horse race on the television, or the dealer's hand in a game of internet blackjack. Take that concentration and let's call it a 'ring fence'.

Use it to guard against other people's cynicism and disbelief, whether that's directed against the illness concept or against a belief that you can change or cure yourself.

Learned helplessness

Does low self-esteem cause gambling? Or is it a result of gambling?

I experienced a loving, secure upbringing and have had an interesting, varied life, so I don't see myself as a natural candidate for low self-esteem. However, both animals and humans can become trained into accepting that they are helpless, unable to change a situation or to change course significantly from the direction they are travelling. The idea of *learned helplessness* – feeling that you have no personal power to change a situation – stems from research with dogs by Martin Seligman at the University of Pennsylvania in 1967, and was quickly extended to human behaviour. It can play a part in all sorts of situations, from sports performance to dealing with trauma.

Learned helplessness accounts for aspects of behaviour that develop over time with compulsive gamblers. They accept that they can't win back their losses; they won't win that jackpot; they won't save their marriage; they will lose their job and so forth if they carry on gambling. They have *learned that they are helpless* to change those odds, and so continue gambling.

Gambling and physical health

There are also ways, however, in which gambling may actually affect your physical health and well-being. I experienced many of these physical symptoms myself:

- Most probably your gambling, as well as all the fallout from it, physically exhausts you on a daily basis. I know it did with me. When I was in the thick of the addiction I was continually tired through not sleeping properly, because I was going to sleep thinking about gambling and waking up (often in the middle of the night, or very early in the morning) thinking about gambling.
- I became hugely stressed by my gambling and what it was doing to me and my life.
- I became hugely overweight because I gave up caring for my body and totally lacked any exercise as it was time away from gambling.

- As a result of that excessive weight and lack of exercise my blood pressure rocketed and I had very high cholesterol.
- I also found that I had begun to drink too much in order to try and blot out what my gambling was doing to me.
- I found I couldn't concentrate on anything other than gambling, whether it was work or a conversation with my wife or any other aspect.

If you still don't think you had an illness, let's imagine you walk into a doctor's surgery and present him with the key symptoms I've just mentioned:

> *Doctor*: What appears to be the problem?
> *Patient*: Well, doctor, I'm suffering from exhaustion, tiredness and stress. I'm overweight and I have high blood pressure and high cholesterol. I'm drinking too much and I can't concentrate.

The above list shows just some of the illnesses and disorders that compulsive gambling can cause. Compulsive gamblers are documented to run a higher risk of experiencing certain health problems, physical and mental.

Physical health suffers because gambling addicts often eat poorly, and also tend to ignore any early signs of illness. One study (Rosenthal and Lorenz, 1992) showed that addicted gamblers may go without sleep or food for days in order to continue gambling. In addition, according to an article published in the *Journal of Gambling Studies* (Christensen, Patsdaughter, Babington), gamblers typically suffer stress-related symptoms such as high blood pressure, headaches, skin problems, and gastrointestinal conditions such as nausea, ulcers and colitis; also mounting debts and strained relationships often lead to insomnia. Other research supports the fact that problem gamblers experience certain physical conditions, including liver disease, high heart-rate and angina: a survey of 43,000 Americans by the University of Connecticut Health Center found that addicted gamblers were twice as likely to have angina and tachycardia (an excessively rapid heartbeat) and three times more likely to have liver disease.

Various studies have found that gambling addiction is associated with high rates of alcoholism and drug abuse, anxiety, depression, antisocial personality disorder, mood disorders and other conditions, leading some researchers to suspect that an addiction to gambling is itself often a symptom of an underlying mental-health problem.

Last but not least, problem gamblers' families also suffer the effects of tension and stress, and may also develop stress-related physical problems. *Do ensure that any member of the family who doesn't feel well goes to the doctor.*

Parkinson's disease

Bizarrely, people with Parkinson's disease are at greater risk of becoming gambling addicts, especially those diagnosed at a younger age, and are particularly vulnerable to online gambling. This appears to be a fairly rare side-effect of the anti-Parkinson's medication dopamine agonists, and is reversible with a change of drug regime. But if you or any member of your family has Parkinson's and is concerned about this, you should consult your doctor.

Assessing your health

At this stage it's a good idea to take stock of your health – and that of your partner and family. Sit down and make a list of how everyone is feeling, physically and mentally.

Again, as the compulsive gambler emerges from the gambling coma, it can be a shock to realize that those around you may be having health and emotional problems related to gambling. Despite you being the cause of those problems, you now need to be the cure for their ills. You can only do that by beginning to mature and becoming strong for them. Caring for them, and thinking of their needs, finally, before your own, is all part of the long-term cure. By helping others, you are regaining pride in yourself, and feeding your soul with positive energy by realizing that there is goodness inside you.

Recap

1 Accept your gambling as an illness.

2 Recognize the 'emotional solitary confinement' that you put yourself into while gambling and use that force to blot out negative comments from others who say you'll never quit gambling.

3 Take a long hard analytical look at your health (mental and physical) and that of those around you, including your partner, if you have one. Make a firm resolution to begin improving your own health in order to help improve that of others.

6

Signposts: dealing with urges

Just as your gambling rolled along slowly at first and then became unstoppable, so your recovery will do the same. If you had managed to stop and think seriously when you were gambling, you probably wouldn't have got to this stage. Likewise we don't want to stop or even slow the momentum of your recovery, as that will give you time to think about gambling.

Imagine your gambling as a giant fortress in which you've been trapped up until now. At this point, you have an option: the draw-bridge goes down over the moat, the castle gates swing open, the light of day enters. What do you do? Walk, or most probably run, as fast and as far as you can.

In such situations, we all want to escape. That's great, but the problem is that all change, even positive change, can be difficult, so we need to guard against those times when we want to turn around and head back to the familiar – that is, the fortress. That is where our key signposts come into play. We need signposts or reminders that point back the way we've just come.

Although you've now confessed to everyone, written a history of your gambling, sent it to those affected and seen your gambling as an illness, this book doesn't suggest that those actions are going to be enough on their own to stop your gambling in its tracks and enable you never to return to it (i.e. relapse). No, it will take a number of strong signposts to remind you of where you have come from – indeed, escaped from. That is what we are going to do now: create your individual signposts to act as potent reminders of the past. You'll be able to refer back to these signposts when you are living in the land of the normal, and maybe they'll be useful to pass on to others, to show how you beat compulsive gambling.

1 Your gambling history

We have already touched on this subject in Chapter 3, but I will explain its importance in the context of being the first signpost you see as you leave the gambling fortress. As I mentioned in that earlier chapter, the aim is to write a brief but complete record of your gambling – when and where you gambled ever since you started – which is then sent to family members and friends.

There are several reasons why you should send this history of your gambling out within the first few days of your Release. First, it puts down in black and white what it has cost you and your family, not just in financial terms, but also in terms of how much of your life gambling has taken from you and those around you. Second, and importantly, it cuts off your easiest source of funding for your gambling. For sure, if your will power is great enough to continue gambling, you will find alternative sources of funds, but none is usually as easy (barring the shame) as tapping close friends and family. That immediately puts some space between you and gambling. Because you have to try harder to fund it, you immediately have some breathing space, which is vital in these early days. Consciously or subconsciously, you are saying to all the people you stole from (as I consider it theft when the money was taken under false pretences), 'Never again lend me money.'

Another benefit of the gambling history is that it helps show others, even at this early stage, that there was something very wrong. You may find that some people try to downplay the gambling, or to disregard the extent of the problem. Sharing it – so long as you are completely honest – allows most non-gamblers to see where your big problems occurred, and then the final slide into gambling oblivion. For me, it was my involvement in online gambling, for you it may be something else.

For many gamblers – or ex-gamblers – this signpost offers their first chance since they stopped gambling to be honest, mature and not entirely selfish. Obsessive gambling has great power to keep people immature, lying continually and thinking of no one other than themselves. Being completely honest with the gambling history and giving other people the chance to see and understand, at least a little, how devastating it was, gives the gambler the chance to show concern for others. The history can act as a tangible sign of good will.

For many, this is an important step on the road to normality. At this early raw stage, many ex-gamblers are desperate to feel that there is some decency left in their souls. This basic self-respect is a vital foundation of recovery and indeed of mental health.

Repentance is all very well, and probably quite acceptable to family and friends in small doses at first – at last the gambler has come to his or her senses! But it mustn't be allowed to swamp the person. If all she is going to do, as a newly recovering compulsive gambler, is blame herself for how bad she's been and what a horrid person she is, then depression can set in, and the low self-esteem nurtured by gambling will raise its head again. All it takes then is a row with a partner or harsh words from a friend to convince the gambler that she can't kick gambling – and she falls right back in there. Both the gambler and those around need physical 'pointers' that in effect say 'Yes, I did make a mess of things, but I'm on the road to recovery. I can be thoughtful, honest and mature.'

As the partner or friend of the compulsive gambler, please try to recognize the courage that it takes a compulsive gambler to write this gambling history and distribute it to all those affected by the gambling. Try not to belittle it, or to be angry at the sheer scale of the problem. What the compulsive gambler is trying to do, as she did while confessing her gambling, is to purge herself of this evil inside her.

◁ 2 ▷ Past bank statements and credit card bills

Signpost 2, the bank statements, clearly helps show all those affected by your gambling the scale of the problem. Signpost 2 is more powerful than Signpost 1, the gambling history, as it has come from the bank itself and so can't be either underplayed or exaggerated. It is there, in black and white. People respect and believe bank and credit card statements.

Bank and credit card statements really highlight how much gambling took over your life. For example, how does a partner feel when she sees that beside her birthday or wedding anniversary is a deposit to the internet casino of X pounds or dollars, or a large cash withdrawal which the compulsive gambler can't explain? Maybe she thinks back to the excuses made at the time as to why the gambler couldn't afford to take her out to celebrate the event that night. Grief and resentment are real possibilities here. Painful as this exercise is, though, it is beneficial. Hang in there.

What the money represented

You need to start putting a face on the money used for gambling. Look at each deposit and think what that amount represents to you, your partner, your family, and even your friends. I'm sure you will see that each deposit represents something negative – at the least, lost opportunities to share with other people what the money could have bought, from a relaxed coffee out to a new outfit for a child or a household bill met on time and peace of mind all round.

For the compulsive gambler's loved ones, going through these bank and credit card statements will doubtless prove very painful as well. That was your money too, and represents a wasted life for you as well as the compulsive gambler. It probably represents compromised friendships and relationships as well as a great deal of actual hardship. It may well remind you of the items (luxuries and necessities) that you have had to go without, and of the emotional pain when you had to shoulder the burden of explaining (or perhaps lying) to children, friends or relatives why you couldn't afford to buy them something, or do something with them.

Looking at deposits can be as painful as looking at withdrawals. Just as you may see the negative aspects of all those withdrawals, and what you went without, so you may also begin the slow realization that the few highlights of recent years strangely tie in with unaccounted-for deposits (i.e. not the monthly salary). It's natural that this will colour your whole view of your relationship over that period. How many of those precious moments that you so enjoyed at the time were determined by the successful roll of a dice, turn of a card, or pick of a horse? Was that unexpected bunch of flowers, the day driving a Ferrari or the weekend away determined by a recent win, or was it done out of true love and affection from your partner? It may be none of them or it may be all, or somewhere in between, but the very fact that you have to think about it taints the memory of that moment or gesture. Were those apparently thoughtful actions what we might call 'emotional credits'? That is, attempts by the compulsive gambler to deposit some warm emotion into his partner's account in order to feel better about himself?

Are you starting to see now the power of this second signpost, the bank and credit card statements? That is what we mean by signposts. Don't you think you would feel the same if you had all your past bank statements sitting there in front of you? Of course you would, so get on the phone now to your bank and credit card providers and ask them to get it organized. My wife even negotiated the cost so that we got the statements for virtually nothing, so give that a try too.

◁ 3 | Time, your most important possession

'Lost, yesterday, somewhere between sunrise and sunset, two golden hours, each set with sixty diamond minutes. No reward is offered for they are gone forever.'

Horace Mann

I have read over and over again, in the books I tried and also in internet chat rooms, that the compulsive gambler must accept that the money lost through gambling is lost for ever and can never be regained. No doubt people writing this mean well, and want you to accept that you can't win back by further gambling the money you have lost through gambling. I accept that, but what a negative statement! You've maybe just stood up physically at a meeting, or metaphorically in an internet chat room, and laid your soul bare to a bunch of strangers, and one of the first messages you receive is that you'll never see that £5,000, £50,000 or £500,000 that you threw away on gambling ever again. As a raw, sulky, petulant compulsive gambler my first reaction would be: What is the point of even trying then? Whatever the amount, it is such a high mountain to climb that you feel you may as well try gambling again in the vain hope that the jackpot will come in.

The first thing for the gambler to accept is that the time you spent gambling and thinking about gambling is the only thing that can't ever be recovered. Time is the most precious commodity we have on this planet. Ask a cancer patient who has two months to live how precious time is. I once read an article about a British man who won £19 million on the Lottery and yet would give it all up to have more time; he had a potentially life-threatening disease that would leave his beloved wife on her own.

You might feel that you have wasted the time you were given, or that your use of time has been stupid and selfish. Or that, even worse, you have stolen the time from those you love, by involving them in your gambling, whether physically, financially or emotionally. Accept that the time was lost gambling, and commit yourself to never wasting a second of the time given to you, on gambling or even thinking about gambling, again.

For this third signpost, I suggest that you sit down and honestly estimate how much time you have spent gambling, just in this past month. Average out the time you spent per day and multiply by the number of days in the month, or just add the hours per day individually. It's up to you. When you have a number of hours that you think is as accurate as you can get it, multiply it by the number of months you have gambled in the last 12 months (probably every month). When you get the total number of hours for the 12 months divide it by 24. With that total write the figure down as the number of days you spent gambling in the past year. This amount only counts the time spent actually gambling. It doesn't include all the time involved in trying to obtain money to gamble, the time spent thinking about your last gamble, the time spent thinking about your next gamble and so forth. For example:

Tom gambled, on average two hours a day this month.
That's 60 hours this month.
This equals 720 hours in the past year.
720 hours equals 30 days.

Take an A4 piece of paper and write in the biggest letters possible:

I wasted 30 days of my life gambling this year and I can *never* get those days back again.

Then write today's date beside it and keep it safe.

Promise yourself and everyone around you *never* to waste another minute gambling. Bring out that page whenever you think you might want to gamble again.

◁ 4 ▷ Accepting you were a hopeless gambler

This is another subject we touched on in Chapter 3, but it is the important last signpost before we move on, so it is worth looking at it again. It intertwines with the other three, because by writing your gambling history, reading your bank and credit card statements and calculating your time lost through gambling, you can only arrive at one conclusion:

You were a hopeless gambler!

If you had been any good you wouldn't be where you are now, reading this. It is that plain, and yet I can still almost hear the voice in your head trying to fight it. Why not admit it and move on?

For this signpost all you need to do is take another A4 piece of paper and write in the biggest letters possible:

I admit I *was* a hopeless gambler

Put today's date on it and keep it in a box along with Signpost 1, your gambling history, Signpost 2, your bank and credit card statements, and Signpost 3, your calculation and statement of the time you have lost gambling. If ever you feel tempted to gamble again, take five minutes out, open up that box and look through your four signposts.

Dealing with urges

You'd think, wouldn't you, that the above would be enough to halt any further thoughts of gambling. But addiction doesn't work like that. It is important to recognize potentially dangerous feelings and emotions during the early days after you have stopped gambling. Depending on its level and depth, your confrontation or confession, or release, may in itself be enough to dispel any notion of gambling again, so that you may find that in those early days the urges aren't there, or that they are only fleeting. However, it is best to be on your guard against such urges, particularly during times of financial pressure when they can raise their ugly head again. Knowing how to handle them and overcome them means they remain harmless urges.

First of all, it is important to recognize an urge to gamble for what it is. It is just an urge, and like all urges it can be resisted. You may have an urge to eat chocolate, or an urge to go up and kiss a beautiful stranger in the street, or to throw off all your clothes and skip naked through a fresh meadow on a sunny spring morning, but it doesn't mean that you have to follow these urges through, and most of us don't (hopefully not the last one, anyway!). Gambling urges are no different. They don't have to be acted on and can, very easily, be overcome, until they've passed.

Trust me, these urges will soon get bored with trying to tempt you back into gambling if you ignore them and attack them, so try to picture them as something physical, which can be broken down and destroyed.

The urges won't necessarily disappear overnight, but it doesn't matter how often you get them, or how intense they are, provided that you have learned to overcome them. Take it as a challenge, and confront them head on. Time is a great healer with these urges and they will eventually die down and completely disappear. But what anyway is there to be scared of, if they remain but you are in control of them?

When you do have a gambling urge:

- Think of another recent, non-gambling-related urge that you had, but resisted. That in itself will reinforce your belief that you can beat your gambling urges. Write it down if it helps.
- Discussing urges with someone else, your partner or a friend, can help to relieve them. This accounts for much of the strength and usefulness of help forums such as GamCare, or group therapy such as Gamblers Anonymous. People are able to write down their urges in such contexts, or even phone them in, and it gets the urge off their chest, and disrupts their pattern enough (from when they were gambling daily and satisfied every gambling urge) for them to overcome those urges.
- Once you have overcome an urge to gamble, particularly a strong one, reward yourself. Treat yourself to a hot bath or a couple of pints at the pub. Go online or phone a friend and tell him or her about it – after all, this is Gamblers Aloud and you are encouraged to be forthright about these things! If you can't find anyone

to share with, then be proud of yourself and walk around with a smile on your face. Be happy with yourself first, and then let others follow and share that happiness.

The Mind Gym

Let's look at the subject of beating your urges from a slightly different perspective. You haven't been into a gym for over two years, but, maybe because it is 2 January and getting fit was one of your New Year's resolutions, you decide to go. You walk in, register, change into your gear and get down to it. Ask yourself something as you imagine this scenario. Are you going to walk up to the weights and immediately try to bench press 220 lb? Are you going to jump on the treadmill, set it to maximum speed and maximum incline and then keep going for 60 minutes solid? Whether you are male or female, I think the answer is going to be no to both options. So why then would you think you can instantly stop having urges to gamble, without training and exercising your mind a little first? You need to train and exercise and build up your mind's strength in just the same way that you need to gently condition and push your body in order to build your physical strength.

Practise having 'dry runs' whereby you imagine that you have a gambling urge, and then go through how you are going to stop it, what you are going to do, and how you are going to think, in order to stop yourself fulfilling that urge.

With this practice and a few successful attempts at resisting those urges you will soon learn the technique and grow mentally stronger, just as by going to the gym, your body becomes better conditioned. I found that by going to the gym *and* conditioning my mind, I very quickly became both mentally and physically stronger and more able to take on my problems as I came out of compulsive gambling. You will find pride in overcoming those urges and the fact that, finally, you are regaining a bit of control in your life.

Recap

1 Create your four signposts in order to remind yourself of your past: your gambling history; your bank and credit card statements; your lost time; and your acceptance that you were a hopeless gambler. Fully recognize and understand that the

greatest loss when you were gambling was *time* and not *money*. Be determined never to waste another minute of your life with gambling or even gambling thoughts and be confident that you will rebuild your finances through hard work and honest toil.

2 Carry out all four signposts with passion and honesty, as these are the key to ensuring that you never gamble again.

3 Learn to recognize urges for what they are, and understand that you don't have to act on those urges. Actively practise and train your mind to overcome those urges in preparation for when you may have them.

7

Restoring your dignity and self-respect

Lucas

A cornerstone of my success in not only stopping gambling, but overcoming even the urge to gamble, and becoming a good person again, was my wife's ability to restore my dignity, so soon after confronting me with my gambling. Within two weeks of my confrontation or release, I could again access the ATM and log on to the internet bank account, and we gave up me keeping every receipt to show every penny that I spent, with the cash that I had. I cannot emphasize how important that was in this entire process, as it was the start of me re-entering the real world and beginning to be a mature adult again.

Compulsive gamblers are basically very immature people. They don't 'do' responsibility, maturity or any sort of financial planning in the same way that 'normal' people do. They have a fervent belief that whatever happens, they'll be able to gamble their way back into the black. We've already discussed the fact that we gamble(d) for many reasons – probably one of the least important is actually to win money, however bizarre that sounds. Whatever the reasons why my gambling became compulsive, I had to accept that my compulsive gambling made and kept me very immature. I feel it also left me cruel and emotionally barren.

Cutting access to finances

It's a common and no doubt natural reaction among family and friends to try to prevent you from having access to the means to start gambling again. A full and frank confession of your gambling, therefore, may well elicit suggestions like the following:

- Cut up your credit cards.
- Cancel the internet banking facility.

- Put your partner in charge of the bank account.
- Pay your salary into your partner's account instead of yours, or the joint account.
- Get your partner to give you only the cash you need on a daily basis, and you must bring receipts back for everything you've bought.
- Tell your partner or friend *exactly* where you are going when you go out and how long you expect to be.
- Install a gambling block on the computer, or even put a prohibition on your unsupervised use of the computer.

Some gamblers find this kind of rigorous programme helpful, indeed necessary for a while, even if it's just a few days, and may feel that it's a visible and useful sign of their willingness to change. Cutting all access to finances, even if it's just for a brief three- or four-day spell, can act as a signal of commitment to a new way of life, marking a pause between the old, irresponsible life, and the new venture of a gambling-free life.

Others may feel, though, that this heavy-handed approach doesn't give them the breathing space they need at this point to gather their dignity and make their own decisions. However immature you, the gambler, feel you've been during your compulsive gambling, or however immature your loved ones feel that you've been, I'm not sure that being treated like a child, just when you're breaking out of your gambling, is really going to help. Imagine being hit with that list of demands so soon after you've finally been honest and brave enough to confess your gambling. In addition, much of this kind of list specifically refers to people who have partners, so that single people have to find extra strength to handle this themselves. And if you are the partner or friend of a compulsive gambler, it is going to take a tremendous amount of your strength and resolve to follow the suggestions on the list above.

Tom
While we went down the route of deprivation for the first three or four days, it was just sending me back into petulant, secretive, compulsive gambler mode. It wasn't teaching, or more importantly offering, me responsibility. It wasn't saying, 'There is a normal life out there and you can be part of it.' It was like being fitted with an electronic SatNav

tracking tag, at a time when I was emotionally very raw. Of course, I had absolutely no right to expect anything else after what I'd put my wife through, but it wasn't going to be the solution. I would have simply found ways around it and then fallen back into gambling, because the 'real world' didn't offer me what I needed, which primarily was some self-respect and responsibility for my actions.

Restoring the gambler's dignity

Every individual and every partnership is different, so only you can be the judge of when or whether to go through with it. If you are both truly committed, however, as you need to be for our system to work, then you will restore your gambler's dignity as soon as you are convinced it is safe to do. In these early days, you need to look for signs in the ex-compulsive gambler that he is maturing, being honest and open and volunteering information rather than having to have it dragged out of him by you.

You might then want to offer him or her access to finance again. This becomes a huge display of trust by a partner towards the ex-gambler. The partner is sending out a message that in effect says, 'The choice is yours. You can reward my trust and not gamble or you can let me, and more particularly yourself, down and go back to your selfish ways and destroy this relationship and most probably the rest of your life.' That, I think, is a pretty powerful message.

To the compulsive gambler I would say, try to recognize what a huge step this is in your overall recovery, and don't underestimate what failure will mean. Some gamblers feel that they have made their partner and family suffer so much that they won't be able to take any more failure or betrayal should they abuse that trust again. This way, your family show they trust you, but are also offering you your dignity back.

Many ex-gamblers are extremely grateful for this opportunity, especially if they feel guilty at the pain they may have caused by their gambling. Others find it humiliating, although if you think about it, you may actually have had less dignity while gambling. It isn't dignified (let alone mature) to borrow money from friends and family, and even less dignified continually to lie about the reasons for each loan. It isn't dignified to sneak out and slip into bookies or casinos, amusement arcades or bingo halls, and afterwards lie to your partner about where you've been. It isn't dignified to skulk into pawn shops and hawk family heirlooms or previous gifts, in order to get a few more pounds to gamble with. Faced with memories of the undignified acts associated with gambling, do you really want to return to that? Hopefully not. For your partner and family to show they trust you with money again offers a chance to restore your dignity even to your pre-gambling days, not just from when you gave up.

Maturing your conscience

Developing a mature relationship with money is part of coming to terms with life after gambling. You know it isn't mature not to have enough money in the bank to pay the mortgage or rent, or to sail so close to the financial wind that one unexpected expense can push you off course, so that you revert to more gambling to try to pay that bill. Mature relationships with others are another issue. Is it a mature relationship that you have with your partner, if you are continually lying to her about your whereabouts, why you took longer than expected, why you forgot something she'd asked you to bring (because you were stuck in the bookie's) and so forth?

Developing a more mature conscience can be a huge step forward in recovery, as well as in establishing relationships that have more mutual respect.

Draw strength from knowing that you'll no longer be supporting the gaming industry, but that you now have the opportunity to do some good in the world. For example:

- For the equivalent of what I'd nonchalantly toss a blackjack croupier after she had dealt me an ace and queen, with £300 sitting on my spot, I can now inoculate an impoverished child against the six main killer diseases.
- For what I'd desperately bet on a 25/1 outsider as a last-gasp effort to recoup the day's losses, I can now feed a kennelful of abandoned dogs at our local shelter for a week.

- With the money I'd blow in one hour online with the internet casino, I can now educate five children in a remote village for one whole year.

That is humility to me. That empowers me never to gamble again. That restores my dignity and my self-respect and feeds the hatred for the industry that courses through my veins and blocks any notion of ever gambling again.

Recap

1 Sit down and discuss the issue of restoring access to finances with your partner.
2 Recognize the second chance you are getting.
3 Work continually on maturing your conscience, and on becoming a kinder, more thoughtful person in the way you use money.

8

The chip of change

Gambling is thought to have evolved from primitive divinatory rituals in prehistoric societies, whose members would use small objects such as stones or sticks to see if they fell out as odd or even (a process known as casting the lots). Small bones such as knucklebones or astragali were also used, whose irregular shape forms a very basic kind of dice, with four large sides and two more rounded sides. Cubic dice dating from around 3000 BC have been found in the Mesopotamia region and from 2000 BC in Egypt. In other words, it looks as though humankind has always used small objects to help steer a way through the chancy game of life. This chapter looks at how to use this ancient instinct to your benefit now that you're recovering.

No doubt you're familiar with casino chips – those apparently harmless, coloured little bits of plastic that are key to blackjack and other forms of competitive gambling. This chapter looks at how to convert this element of the gaming system into part of your own recovery system, so that it becomes a powerful personal symbol that acts as a physical reminder of gambling.

Of course, you might have some other token that you find works best for you. There's absolutely no intrinsic value in the chip itself, but this exercise shows how to harness the power of habit and make it work for you. Just as you used chips – or maybe other private tokens – in your gambling, so this chapter looks at how to make the props of your gambling life work for you in your gambling-free life.

The chip is integral to the overall success of your recovery. Just because it is relatively small and simple, please don't discard its power or effectiveness. In so many aspects of life, we overcomplicate things. If you do nothing else other than keep this chip with you at all times, without losing it, this alone represents a huge change from your gambling behaviour and attitude, and that is what we are trying to achieve throughout this system: break up your routine; change your mindset; clear your head of negativity; remind yourself of how you were but at the same time, get you living your life for today and the future.

The principle of the chip

The idea of the chip of change came about from something that I did during the first few days after I'd stopped gambling. I started carrying around a special coin, and would often find myself running it across the back of my fingers, as I'd done with casino chips while playing blackjack in a casino. If you watch televised poker matches you will see nearly all the players doing exactly the same thing with their stack of chips, or with an individual chip.

At other times, I would toss the coin and mentally call 'heads' or 'tails' to see how long a successful run I could achieve until the inevitable loss. Much of this initially seemed to be almost subconscious, in that I wasn't really aware I was doing it. After a few days, I realized that the coin was becoming a kind of 'comfort blanket'. As time went on and I remained gambling-free, and as even the urge to gamble was disappearing fast, the same coin grew in importance and I started taking even more care of it. I can say with certainty that if you were to meet me on the street today I could still pull out that same special coin from my right-hand pocket.

What I am doing with this chip is basic reverse psychology. Nothing clever, nothing smart, just taking something that represented a very negative aspect of your life (your gambling) and turning it into a very positive aspect of your life (your control and your choice). The great thing is that the benefit doesn't end there. This chip is a small but constant anchor, a tangible reminder of how ultimately with gambling you will always lose in the end but how also you can be in control of your life. Let's now look at these and other benefits in more detail.

Benefit 1: A reminder that you always lose in the end with gambling

Tossing a coin is about the simplest form of gambling there is. If you always keep a chip with you, you can, in your quiet times, call 'heads' or 'tails' to yourself as you flip the chip. Maybe you'll lose the first time and give up. Maybe you'll call correctly five times in a row, 'doubling or quitting' each time, but ultimately you may not stop until you lose. That was what was wrong with your gambling. That is what got you where you are today. Almost certainly you were affected by what is recognized as 'the gambler's fallacy'. This means that you try to defy the laws of chance and probability, for example by thinking that because the coin has landed heads three times in a row, the chances are that the next flip will come up tails. Sorry, but the odds that the coin will land heads or tails are identical for every single flip of the coin, irrespective of the previous result. It's this kind of thinking that often leads gamblers to chase their losses and get deeper into trouble, as they just can't believe that their bad luck will continue. That is the 'fallacy', as you have no doubt found out on countless occasions, to your enormous cost!

The chip in your pocket serves as a continual reminder of the fact that, sooner or later, you lose. It's simple but effective. I defy you not to have a fleeting spike of disappointment as your run comes to an end, even though you don't have one cent riding on it. There is then a warm glow of pleasure and contentment as you realize you've cracked it. It meant nothing. I lost nothing. What an idiot I was to have my life revolve around the flip of that coin or its equivalent: the turn of a card, the fall of a roulette ball, the call of a bingo number.

Benefit 2: Finally, you are in control

The second great healing power of your chip is that it symbolizes your control over your life and your emotions. When you have one in your pocket, as you are rolling it over your fingers, it is you who have the power to decide which side is facing up. When you flip it, as I explained above, and when you gamble, then immediately you are no longer in control of how it will land. That is in the hands of fate or chance or luck or randomness, or whatever you wish to call it. It might seem too simplistic to you, but who else is in control (or out of control) of your life if not you?

So take that chip now, turn it over the back of your fingers and have a long hard think: in control or out of control . . . negative mood or positive mood . . . bad past or great future . . . selfish and conceited or compassionate and generous . . . and so forth. It is entirely up to you what good and bad you want the chip to represent, but it is giving you that *choice*. Something you maybe never had while in the grip of your addiction and illness.

Benefit 3: Money in your pocket

The chip can also represent money in your pocket. It is a 'comfort blanket'. If I have the chip, then I have something. This again sounds incredibly simple, because it is. How many times have you, say, walked through wet streets after the casino closed because you hadn't even kept enough money for a taxi or train ride home? How many times did you leave a betting shop without even enough money for a sandwich to replace the lunch that you missed? Quite a few if you were anything like me! With the chip in your pocket, it's a reminder that you always have something. If you are following the system outlined in this book, you'll have more besides just the chip. You'll start having a bit in the bank, a few less debts and far less stress. That is what that chip represents in your pocket.

Benefit 4: A 'lucky charm' – dealing with superstitious thoughts

In the few clinical studies that have been conducted on compulsive and problem gamblers, it has been found that they place a disproportionate amount of faith in luck and lucky charms – part of their so-called 'magical thinking'. Now I know that that statement isn't going to have you falling off your chair in disbelief. I'm sure all of us have lucky numbers for roulette or the lottery, lucky slot machines, only bet on horses with names we relate to, or – even worse (and I promise you, I have done this) – bet on a horse I was convinced winked at me in the paddock! I'm sure you have no end of other bizarre quirks, which convince you that you are one of 'the lucky ones'. Unfortunately, the cold fact is that if we were, I wouldn't have needed to write this book, and you certainly wouldn't need to be reading it.

So, another benefit of the chip is that it can now represent the 'luck' you had finding this system and beating gambling. Of course, it isn't just going to take luck to beat it. It's going to take a lot of willpower, determination and some pain. That chip in your pocket is a constant little reminder that you're fighting the battle, and no longer relying on 'luck' to get you through life.

Benefit 5: A badge of honour

This might sound a bit bizarre, but why not see the chip as a tangible sign that you have committed to giving up gambling for ever? As stated in Chapter 7, there are reasons why you might want to come clean about your gambling, and not take the 'anonymous' approach. While the chip may be a secret, kept in your pocket it can act as your own personal badge of honour. Who knows, in time it may come to mean something to others too.

Benefit 6: Money is important – look after it

As I said earlier, forging a mature relationship with money is an integral part of your recovery process. Many gamblers show a remarkable carelessness and recklessness not just with their own money, but with that of their partner, family, friends, even the bank. It's common to be blind to the everyday value and use of money, and to the good causes to which it could have been put. What the negative side (the clouds) of one of those chips in your pocket represents is all that, and much more. The positive side (the sun) represents your thoughtfulness to others, your compassion and humility, your laughter, your strength, your willpower. Put the two sides together and they represent *your choice*.

Keeping it with you

For the chip to be effective, it's best to take it with you everywhere. That means that you cannot leave the chip in your trouser pocket when your jeans go to the wash. You can't leave for work in the morning with the chip left on the bedside table. You can't get up from a sofa and allow the chip to fall down between the cushions. You can't include the chip in a bunch of loose change you leave on a dish as a tip for a waitress. You have to stop and think. Where is my chip?

So there you go! There are six powerful benefits to carrying a chip or similar small token around with you. It's an effective part of our approach in that it is non-intrusive – it is there with you constantly, representing these six benefits, and yet it allows you to get on with your gambling-free life. It does so much more for you than a daily diary and yet requires you to do so much less.

Don't leave home without it!

Recap

A simple one:

Never, ever, be without your chip!

9

The futility and danger of gambling

If you're the gambler, this chapter requires you to do some serious contemplation and really look inside yourself. It would be beneficial to study it with your partner or friend if available. You should be fresh, calm and relaxed before entering into it. Although by now, if you are following the steps in this book, you will have stopped gambling, this chapter asks you to pause again and seriously to reflect on two routes your life can now take. The aim – and it's an important one – is to anchor firmly in your mind the futility and danger of gambling, so that you continually commit yourself to never going back to it.

If you're the partner or friend of the gambler, it would be helpful if you could arrange to work through this exercise with your gambler. It's a powerful exercise which uses imagination and visualization to consider in some detail how the gambler's future life might go.

If you're the gambler, what I suggest you do right now, is if you have a favourite armchair, go and sit in it. Make a cup of tea or cocoa, or have a cold beer. Sit in your favourite chair, relax and think of yourself at the age of 80. Sure, if you continue to gamble, there's a reasonable chance you will have topped yourself before then (sorry to be brutal but it's a fact), but at least try.

Try picturing the scenarios that follow and then adapt them to your own personal circumstances.

Scenario 1

You are 80, sitting comfortably in the same chair, remembering the day you read this book. You remember that you made one last promise to yourself, that you would never gamble again and that you really would give the advice in this book a go. Today was different; you'd tried Gamblers Anonymous, and while you had always managed to stay off gambling for a week or occasionally a month, you had always slipped back, for one reason or another. Well, that day *was* different, and you never did gamble again. Not only that, but you never wanted to gamble again, never felt the urge to gamble. You awoke from a gambling 'coma' and saw what a wasteful occupation gambling was, how cruel it was to so many people, as well as to the hundreds of thousands of beautiful horses and dogs helplessly involved in it. You recognized how cruel it had been to you and those you loved. You knew that in your heart you weren't a cruel person, and so you were able to accept that it was gambling that made you cruel. You accepted that you had an illness but that the cruel and heartless gambling industry had fed that illness, as tobacco companies create, feed, encourage and nurture smokers and alcohol companies create, feed, encourage and nurture drinkers.

The gambling industry, backed by your own government, had depicted gambling as a fun, acceptable activity that might provide you with untold wealth. They'd seduced you with introductory offers, made gambling an everyday activity, dressed your favourite football stars in the logos of internet gambling companies. Those companies had been allowed to advertise everywhere, the internet casino business had been encouraged to flourish. How could all that be allowed if it then caused you so much pain?

The great thing about that day was that a cure came along for that illness and from that day you never did gamble again, or feel the urge to gamble. Sure, it didn't begin to rain 24-carat gold leaves from the sky and you weren't instantly rich. Sure, you didn't overnight become the perfect wife or husband, mother or father, son or daughter, but you felt better in yourself. You were able to look yourself in the mirror and say 'Hey, I had an illness, but I'm over it. I couldn't help it.' Then a little smile creased the corners of your mouth, and finally, after so many years, you said to yourself in the mirror, 'I could learn to love you a little.' Amazingly, once you'd done that, other people started liking you and loving you more. Even your close family and friends, who never stopped loving you but couldn't understand you, couldn't understand how you could hurt them so much through this ridiculous gambling addiction!

From that day on, life just got better. There was a little less financial strain now you weren't gambling. Things were worked out with the card companies, banks and building societies. You remember being amazed at how understanding they'd all been. Being the old cynic you are, you soon realized that they were just interested in getting something back from you, rather than seeing you thrown in jail, but what did you care? Quickly you began getting your pride and dignity back because, despite whatever anyone else said or thought, you knew that you had had an illness, and couldn't help it. That was your strength. You soon even began to laugh at how stupid you'd been to gamble and then you began to hate the industry, in all its forms. Now that you had a little spare cash, you actually began to do good things for other people, as well as those close to you. You were learning humility!

Your tea has probably gone cold now, or your beer has got warm, so why not make a fresh cup or get a cold one from the fridge, before we look at Scenario 2?

Scenario 2

Now imagine that you aren't sitting in the same chair, because they came and repossessed it a couple of years back. You are actually sitting in a shelter for the homeless as they've allowed you a bed for the night, after you'd slept on the streets for the past fortnight. Inevitably, as it has done so often in the intervening years, your mind turns back to the day when you were reading this book about this new system, in the comfort of your own home. It was a Saturday around 6 p.m. You remember your partner curled up on the sofa beside you, contentedly watching a movie, and your teenage daughter excitedly getting herself ready for a night out with her friends. It slices your soul to remember your fear when you surveyed that little vignette. That was your little world. Not perfect by a long shot, but yours.

You were worried, terrified in fact, that you were risking it all by continuing to pursue the gambling addiction that was taking over your life. Its barbs were cutting deeper into your side with every passing day. You knew you were out of control, but you felt powerless to change it. You weren't doing it for fun and yet you literally couldn't stop it. You couldn't talk to anyone as they wouldn't understand. How could they understand it, if you couldn't understand it yourself?

Your partner knew, of course, that something was up, but you had kept it from him or her so well up to that point. The house had already been remortgaged and you were already one month behind on the repayments. You were maxed out on all your credit cards and none of your family or friends were prepared to lend you even enough to get you to the next pay day. They'd been conned and lied to so many times before that they knew something was up. You were on your final warning at work about taking over-extended lunch breaks because you were spending two hours in the bookie's or the casino, and it felt as if the walls were closing in. You remember your daughter's disappointment at the holiday being cancelled last week, and you match it against her undiluted joy when you walked in having had that big win and splashed out on a surprise holiday for all of you. Was that the last hug you ever got from her? What would you give to feel that unconditional love again? Or for your partner to give you one of those looks and the eyes that promised there was more to come later? How could you have let it get so bad? How could it ever have got so out of control?

You remember, as though it were yesterday, the ring of the door bell as your best friend pitched up at the front door, offering to take you out for an early evening drink. That was your code word for an hour at the bookie's or the casino. How pathetic was that, at your age, using a code word to go gambling? You always wondered why your friend never had your problems with gambling. Why he actually seemed to enjoy gambling. Your friend was cool. Your friend was relaxed. Sure, he didn't stake what you did, didn't bet on every race like you did, never touched the virtual racing or used the fixed odds betting terminals or the slot machines like you did, but was he so different? It didn't seem fair to you that he could enjoy his gambling and didn't have to lie about where he was going, while all it did to you was torture you. You resented your friend for that, even though he was your best friend, but if your friend was your pass to more gambling opportunities then you would stick with him.

Little did you know that session was the catalyst that would spiral you into where you are today – a shelter for the homeless. How were you expected to know your partner would have that little accident in the car after she'd dropped your daughter off at her party? You were going to reinsure the car on Monday, if you had won enough when you were out with your friend that night. You didn't think she would be arrested for driving an uninsured car, but then again you didn't think about anything other than gambling.

Well, it all came out after that. You couldn't even find enough money to bail your partner out or pay the fine and she's never forgiven you for that. Your partner walked out with your daughter, and both your house and your heart were left with a gaping emptiness. Sure enough, you lost your job on the Monday as you were so tied up with the accident and, as they say, the rest is history. Losing the house, a succession of less and less well-paid jobs until literally no one would employ you and no one wanted to know you. You actually became the tramp that you used to sneer at if he came too close in the bookie's, offering you stupid tips in the hope of some charity if the horse actually came in.

Couldn't you just have said, 'No thanks, not tonight. I'm reading this new book and system on giving up gambling'? Couldn't you have had the courage, for once, to have done that? To protect your family, to begin easing their pain, to protect what little you had, to begin being the parent and partner you once were and to commit yourself to rebuilding your life?

Create your own scenario

Read these two scenarios carefully and attentively. Now try to picture your own scenarios. Think them through in as much detail as possible, really visualizing what it might be like. Write it down on a piece of paper if you find that helpful. If you're the gambler's partner or friend, see if it helps to talk it through at this point.

Only you know how bad your gambling got, so be honest with yourself. Even if you've followed the book and the system so far, maybe you have only been going through the motions because your partner or friend bought it for you. Maybe you've retained the compulsive gambler's thinking (dare I say, arrogance) in that you think you can still gamble your way out of this because you are a good gambler. You know you can't get out of it yourself. You know you are one of the unlucky ones who doesn't enjoy their gambling and simply cannot win, and keep those winnings, when those around you can. Nothing will change that, if you start gambling again. You cannot control your gambling. Admit it and admit it now. You know where you are heading if you don't do something, so commit. Commit now, to giving this a go.

Give yourself the opportunity at least to sit down, clear your head, and really think where gambling took you and what sort of person it turned you into. I have seen and read stories on online forums of university students whose lives, just as they are beginning, are being ruined by gambling. I have read accounts from kids as young as 14 and 16, who shouldn't even be allowed to be gambling, having their lives virtually snuffed out by the industry. Get angry for those young people; get angry at the industry that allows such a thing to happen and doesn't put sufficient checks in place to verify their age before they start gambling. You can help stop that happening by giving up gambling yourself. You can at the very least feel better by not supporting an industry that can destroy a young life before it has had a chance to flower, in just the same way that drink or drugs can.

You don't have to be a mathematician or financial wizard to see that gambling is in danger of destroying your finances. It may set you back 10 or 15 years, or even permanently, from achieving your financial goals, such as owning your own house, buying a new car, putting your children through college, securing private health care for your family, investing for your retirement and so forth.

For many who have gone through the torment of gambling, such normal, mature considerations remain dreams. Gamblers live from day to day, finding barely enough to live off, yet finding enough to gamble with. And that is just what gambling does to the problem gambler financially. Let me remind you of some other aspects of life which can be massively affected by gambling. You may well have experienced some of these already, so try making your own list, either alone or with the help of your partner or friend – indeed, if you're the gambler's loved one, you may be able to write it all too easily. Or, make a list each and then compare the two.

- Your ambition will be sucked out of you by gambling. You won't be pushing for promotion or going after a better-paid job any longer. Providing you have enough money to live and gamble with, you will stay within this comfort zone. What potentially is even more serious is that you may even begin to steal or misappropriate funds from work to fund your gambling. That inevitably will lead to you being fired. How stupid is that?

- Besides the immense immediate financial strain that gambling puts on you, there is the long-term damage that it does to you, particularly in terms of your credit rating. Everything from taking out a mobile phone contract and buying a TV on credit, to trying to arrange a mortgage or finance a new car, will become difficult if not impossible. It is likely that this damage will extend to your partner as well if you were financing the gambling from a joint account. How unfair is that?

- You will lose touch with your closest friend, or your spouse or partner, to such an extent that you will hardly recognize him or her and he or she will hardly recognize you. It is quite possible that both parties will resent each other. The gambler resents the non-gambler for the time that has to be spent with them, away from gambling; the non-gambler resents the moody 'shadow' that inhabits the house. So you end up destroying what was probably a very loving and deep relationship through your gambling. How cold is that?

- If you have children, as with your partner, you will begin to lose touch with them and resent them. They will be confused and hurt by this change in their parent and quite possibly blame themselves while not understanding what they've done wrong. How cruel is that?

- You will see less and less of your family, as once again it is time and money spent away from gambling. In the brief spells out of the gambling 'coma', you may have pangs of embarrassment about the lies you have to tell them and the image you must portray to them to keep your gambling secret. It's also possible that if you have been borrowing from friends and family to fund your gambling, without your spouse's knowledge, you will want to keep some distance between them to protect your sources. How evil is that?

- Your health can do nothing other than suffer dramatically through compulsive gambling. Not only will you not have the finances to retain your gym membership, you will also resent time spent exercising, and your motivation won't be there. You know you are draining your life mentally with your gambling, so what is the point in maintaining it physically? The stress levels you put yourself through, either while actually gambling or because of the issues your gambling causes, will be enough to kill you. Inevitably the stress, and your over-active mind, will not allow proper sleep, which will only compound your problems. With poor sleep will come a lack of interest in sex, which will further worsen your relationship with your partner. So your gambling is actually leading you to an early grave. How dangerous is that?
- Your moral fibre will be worn thin through gambling. You probably began your gambling as an upright, honest citizen who wouldn't dream of stealing from others, lying to those closest to you or supporting an industry that abuses animals. Through your gambling, all your values are eroded until the only thing that matters is the gambling. This can often lead to either jail or suicide and sometimes both. How wasteful is that?

With all the above in mind, do you really want and need to start gambling again? From this list, do you recognize any similar changes in yourself since becoming a compulsive gambler? Really ask yourself, 'Is that what I want?' With self-belief, and firm conviction, you can turn your life around. Accept that that was the person you *were*, and move forward to the person you want to be.

Affirmations

The good news is that, even if any of the above has already happened, you can take steps to reverse it. Don't be overwhelmed – I said steps, not that it all has to be done in one go. One useful exercise is to write or record affirmations about how you would like your life to be. Again, both the gambler and his or her loved one may benefit from doing this, either separately or together.

Go back to Scenario 1 and Scenario 2, and reread both carefully – if you or your partner have written your own, so much the better.

Identify where you need to make affirmations. From your scenario, pull out five key areas where you have aims and ambitions, for example the money, love, work, relationships, self-respect.

Make them positive. Avoid using the words 'not' and 'never'. Use the present tense and write as if what you wish for is already happening.

Use your first name.

Write them out ten times each every day, or record them, or both. For example:

I, Tom, am creating financial stability in my life.

I, Tom, am attracting a loving, trusting and relaxed relationship with my partner.

I, Tom, trust myself to give to others and to create basic trust of me in their lives.

I, Tom, get through my work to the best of my ability, bit by bit.

You may have particular goals:

I, Tom, now pay the bank back the £7,000 I owe.

I, Tom, take my family on holiday this July.

Recap

1 Consider carefully the two scenarios offered in this chapter.
2 Create similar scenarios that reflect your own circumstances.
3 List some of the ways in which your life was adversely affected by your gambling, and consider whether you want to go back to them.
4 Make affirmations that express the goals you want to achieve in your new, gambling-free life. Write them out, or record them, ten times a day.

10

The importance of humility and compassion

'Humility is like underwear; essential, but indecent if it shows!'

Humility is a key concept that is crucial to total recovery, so that we never return to gambling. Being compassionate towards other people, thinking of others before yourself, and never compromising someone else's or an animal's life, perhaps by choosing to donate to charity rather than throwing your money away gambling once again, may feel very alien to people at an early stage of recovery. I think it is fair to say that in most of its forms, gambling is a solitary affair even when not at the compulsive stage. While some people might go as a group to the horse or dog races, or a few friends might get together for a night at a casino or the local bingo hall, many if not most gamblers go on their own, as individuals. Even if they start as part of a group going to a casino, there is a strong tendency for them to split off and play favourite tables or slots by themselves, withdrawing into their own gambling world.

A new relationship with money

If you're the ex-compulsive gambler and the principal breadwinner, using money may need some rethinking, and it may take time to relearn that the money is for both of you and the good of your family unit. Some new ex-gamblers may feel that now they're not gambling, and seem to have a little more cash around, they can shower their partners with surprise gifts. Well intentioned though this may be, partners and family won't always (if ever) be impressed. They've learned to be wary of displays of spending, and may feel that it still displays the arrogance and selfishness of the active gambler, who is still acting as if he has the right to spend that money buying gifts. This can be a hard pill to swallow, but hopefully the gambler is now learning not just restraint in money matters, but how to give in less tangible ways. It might help to discuss the kind of gifts that are acceptable – gifts of time, for example, or little jobs done round the house.

There are many bridges that need to be rebuilt on this road to recovery, as well as some routes that you used to take, such as extravagantly splashing out, that you need to avoid travelling on for a long while, if ever. It is much more powerful and compassionate, and shows you are learning humility, if you wait for your partner to offer to indulge you a little, either just for himself or herself or for the two of you.

Lucas
Most active compulsive gamblers rarely, if ever, do anything that benefits anyone else, either emotionally, financially or physically – they're usually too busy doing the exact opposite. I became an immensely selfish person while gambling, and here are just some of the examples.

I would leave my wife alone, late at night, while I was at the casino (we had seven burglaries, including an attempted one on ourselves, in our street in eight months). I freely borrowed money from my ageing parents to fuel my gambling with no thought of what they had to sacrifice (such as holidays, medical bills and the option of going private) to lend me the money. I borrowed money from friends and family but excluded my wife from knowing and therefore compromised her relationship with them.

I left my wife with cancelled private health cover while living abroad. I prevented my wife from travelling (through lack of funds) with me on many trips. I compromised my wife's relationship with her children by not having sufficient funds for them to fly out to visit their mother. And I affected our relationships with immediate family through often being unable to afford Christmas and birthday presents or flights back for special occasions.

Building your recovery – helping others

If you're the gambler, bear in mind that we build our recovery around doing the opposite of what we were doing while being a compulsive gambler. In this case, this means thinking of others' needs first rather than our own. And one of the best ways to turn your focus from yourself to others is to find practical ways of helping other people. This transformation isn't going to happen overnight, either mentally or physically. Mentally you won't suddenly turn into Mr or Mrs Nice, thinking of everyone before yourself, and physically you won't have the finances to help many other people before yourself. So take it step by step, as indicated in the following list. Obviously, the more of these things you can do, and the more committed you are, the quicker and deeper your recovery will be.

If you're the gambler's partner, you might want to be involved with this list. The gambler is used to making money and other decisions in a solitary, not to say secretive, way, and simply having another person involved helps create a whole new healthy dynamic.

- Begin by considering what others around you would like to do today, not what you would like to do. If you're the gambler's partner, you might like to suggest some long overdue activities, such as taking a walk together, visiting in-laws, helping with a project, or making a decision about a child's education.
- Offer to do at least two unpleasant tasks per day around the house that ordinarily (i.e. when you were gambling) you wouldn't have done. You might take out the rubbish, wash up, go food shopping or walk the dog in the rain; it's up to you both. Again, partners may be able to make one or two suggestions!
- At least once a week, take some time to help someone outside your immediate family. It might be an elderly neighbour or wheelchair-bound person who needs some difficult chores doing, or a charity or animal sanctuary that needs a little assistance. It might be manual or administrative work, it doesn't matter. The benefit is that first, you are beginning to put other people first, before yourself, and second, you are starting to use your time in a positive rather than negative manner.
- At least once a month, after you have treated those closest to you, find a little cash, even if it is just £5, to give to a charity or someone in need. Try to budget so that you have enough to give a little. Whatever the amount, it will do you a power of good, and goes a long way to heightening your self-esteem and restoring pride in yourself. As with the saying at the start of this chapter, you don't need to go displaying your underwear every-where – you don't need to go telling everyone you've given to

charity. Just feel good about yourself, and if other people notice, that's great.

The object of this exercise is to stop you thinking only about yourself (as you did when you were gambling) and start you thinking about others (now you've stopped gambling), so as to build humility and compassion.

'Just for today . . .'

'Just for today' is a well-known catchphrase in 12-step programmes such as those used by Gamblers Anonymous and Alcoholics Anonymous. Because many people find the prospect of giving up their obsession for good frightening, if not impossible, this phrase aims to focus them on the present. 'One day at a time' is another popular saying in such groups. 'Just for today I won't gamble' is an aim that some people find more manageable than 'I will never gamble again', and sometimes it can be cut down to 'Just for this morning/the next hour/minute I won't gamble' if things get really tough.

With Gamblers Aloud, we take a different approach which aims to take the focus right away from the gambler and his or her needs. The problem with this phrase is that it implies that the compulsive gambler is only, or at least primarily, thinking of himself or herself. Certainly a partner or friend may benefit indirectly from a gambling-free day, but that is not what we are after!

For the gambler, by refocusing yourself on to other people's needs and desires, especially those closest to you to start with, you are changing your thought processes and even your character from your gambling days. That is a long-term and, to our way of thinking, more permanent cure.

In the 'Just for today' approach the focus and the key word is 'I'; in the same way as when you gambled every day, everything revolves around you. Why not change it to:

Just for today, I will think of someone else first before me.

By doing this, you have a really good chance of rekindling your loved ones' trust and warmth towards you, and they will begin seeing you once more as a caring, sharing person whom they want to be around. I'm not reinventing the wheel when I proclaim that compulsive gamblers need to find something new to focus their lives on after they give up gambling, but where I know our approach is different, is that the refocusing becomes part of the recovery process because it revolves around compassion and humility.

Mary
Without being a goody two-shoes, I think it's vital to find something humane to focus on as early as possible in your recovery. For me, I believe one of the most powerful therapies is to get involved with the RSPCA or one of the greyhound or racehorse rescue and rehoming charities, and begin helping those animals that previously, through gambling, one indirectly may have assisted in abusing and even killing. [See Chapter 12, 'Cruel facts about a cruel industry'.] Forming a bond with an individual animal or animals, by helping walk them and showing them the affection they might never have enjoyed during their brief racing span, and seeing those names on betting slips as living, breathing creatures of beauty with poise and personality, strengthens the resolve of even the hardest heart not to gamble again. We want to put a wet nose and a wagging tail on the crumpled betting slip that previously you threw on the floor of the bookie's without a thought for anyone or anything other than what you had just lost! Even if you never bet on a greyhound in your life before, but were still a compulsive gambler, this is still very powerful therapy.

Getting involved in any form of charitable work, even if it's just giving an elderly neighbour a hand or spending time with someone with their own set of problems, rather than volunteering for a registered charity, will be an immense help to you, as well as those you help. You help yourself by helping others.

The Tree of Humility

We are now going to move on to a little exercise called the Tree of Humility. Ideally this should be done with your partner or friend, but it can also be done just as effectively by yourself. If you feel a bit shy about doing this, you might prefer to do it yourself first, and then consult your loved one as to which parts he or she thinks are

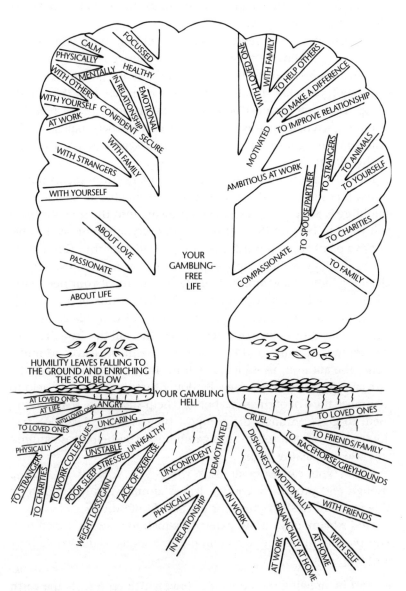

Figure 10.1 The Tree of Humility

true, which parts are exaggerated or underplayed, and anywhere you might have undersold yourself. Study the example in Figure 10.1 before attempting your own.

The baseline or earth represents the 'gambling coma' you were in once your gambling had reached the compulsive level.

Everything below that level represents the roots, gouging through the rot of your life, heading ever closer to hell and the underworld. That may sound like a 1950s horror movie, but I mean it! Gambling's tentacles affect every part of your personality by the time you have got to this stage and keep dragging you further and further down.

Everything above the line (i.e. after you emerge from the gambling coma) is positive and shows how your personality will change after gambling is gone. It represents you growing into the sort of person you want to be, and the sort of person everyone wants you to be. Just as a plant grows towards the sun through phototropism (I knew O level biology would help me one day!), so you grow towards the gleaming light of a gambling-free life. The trunk of your new, gambling-free life is humility, which enables us to think of others first, a kind of thinking which maybe never took place while gambling.

If we take the analogy of a tree further, then all the growth above the ground, in trunk and branches, will result in leaves forming. Come the autumn, those leaves fall to the ground and enrich the earth and soil around the tree. By doing that they not only help to neutralize the evil of the roots but also help any young trees around them to grow, through the compost they produce. Likewise, you don't just help yourself to stop gambling – you help those around you also, by passing it on.

Again, you can only do this when you yourself are strong enough and producing enough leaves annually, as it were, to be able to afford to shed some, for the benefit of others.

Find a blank piece of A4 paper on which to draw your own tree. This picture isn't going to end up in the National Gallery – it's only for you.

- Start by drawing the horizontal line, which represents the earth and your gambling coma.

- Next, draw the roots going down, so that you recognize what gambling turned you into and how it blighted your character. As I said above, you can either do this by yourself or in discussion with your partner or friend. Once you've put down everything you think gambling did to you, move onwards and upwards. It doesn't matter if you forgot some roots, they can always be added on.

- Now add the branches. This may actually be the more difficult bit to do. Put down all the things you like about yourself – or liked in the past. You may have to dig deep if you're still feeling raw and ashamed of yourself. Add in your aspirations and goals. Depending on where you are, reforging trust with others may form an important few branches. Add more branches showing how you feel you have changed and where ultimately you want to end up. Try to think of a key subject – 'Proud', for example – and then branch off from it into what benefits it would bring you. For me it was 'Successful in Love' and 'Successful in Work'. What that is saying is that my pride is being restored through stopping gambling, and that is beginning to make me more successful in my work environment and my love environment (by the latter I mean that I am becoming more caring and attentive towards my wife).

Recap

1 Begin taking practical action to help others in order to build humility and compassion. Consider today what those around you would like to do; offer to do two (or more) unpleasant tasks around the house each day; offer to help someone outside your family once a week; give a little cash to charity at least once a month.

2 Complete your Tree of Humility and begin living by it.

11

Where your money went! Anchoring your hatred of the gambling industry

'The world needs anger. The world often continues to allow evil because it isn't angry enough.'

Bede Jarrett

In this chapter I want to highlight some pretty frightening facts about gambling and the gambling industry, and to show how by its very nature it's stacked against you.

The gambling industry in Great Britain is 'substantial', with a turnover of £84 billion, according to the Gambling Commission. Where does this money go? While some goes on industry maintenance and salaries, a good proportion ends up in the pockets of those in the higher echelons of the industry. The government also collects annual tax revenues of around £2 billion from gambling.

Your list of nothing

To get the maximum effect from this exercise, loved ones should go through it with the gambler. Between you, write down everything that, through your gambling, you don't have but would like to have, and everything you honestly think you have gone without this year because of your gambling. If you have no one, then it is equally effective to sit and write down yourself everything you've missed out on thanks to your gambling. For example:

- holidays
- Christmas presents
- mortgage payments
- a newer car
- treats and outings, such as taking the family to the zoo or cinema
- new clothes or shoes

- the lost romance of a stolen weekend in a cosy hideaway
- a surprise dinner out just to say 'I love you'
- a child's gleeful hug at a mystery present.

Include anything which you couldn't afford because of your gambling.

You need to be honest with each other but also calm. This isn't a time for intense, open anger. Hopefully some of that has passed by now. It is a time for you both to forge a strong hatred of the gambling industry, because of how it has affected you as a couple and/or family. It is far more effective in this chapter that you both get angry at the industry, not the compulsive gambler. You don't need to bring in theories that the compulsive gambler didn't have to gamble, or that the gambling industry was only providing a service or the croupier couldn't be expected to stop you gambling. All of that is totally irrelevant at this stage. If the gambling industry wasn't there, you wouldn't have become a compulsive gambler. Furthermore, the gambling industry does no good to anyone, anywhere. Its sole purpose in life is to make lots of people poor for the sake of making a few people very rich.

This can be a painful exercise. Right now, the compulsive gambler may only be seeing what gambling did to him or her today. He can't process yesterday, last year, ten years ago. This exercise shows in black and white the source of his pain and the life that has been wasted, just as the past bank statements did, and can be very distressing. It is however very valuable.

Profits from the gambling industry

Now take your list and compare it with the profits made by the gambling industry. You can find such information online quite easily these days; start with the basic finance pages of Yahoo or similar search engines. Cold hard gambling industry figures are available to anyone for verification, showing the value of the leading figures in the UK gambling industry, as well as their ranking among the UK's leading companies. These gambling profits are, quite literally, money taken from your pocket. The list you've just compiled is your contribution to this industry, and many compulsive gamblers and their families may feel with some justification that they've given with a lavishness they'd never dream of giving even to their favourite charity. Hopefully, researching this yourself will help reinforce your commitment to giving up.

The ex-compulsive gambler may feel that hatred of the gambling industry doesn't come purely because of the money that he lost to them and the financial hardship it caused him and those around. It comes through the lost opportunities in life caused by the spirit, willpower, sense of adventure and daring being wrung out of the gambler by the compulsion to gamble.

Tom

It was the person I became during my gambling that I hated, and I hate the gambling industry for creating him. During my gambling 'peak' I felt myself being sucked into a moral abyss. I became more and more dishonest and untrustworthy in every aspect of my life. I wasn't just dishonest with my emotions but I physically became dishonest – I was beginning to accept backhanders for orders placed or increasing the price we would buy products for from suppliers in order to include a cut for me. All this was to fuel the gambling habit, and was something I had never entertained doing before. I despised people who reduced themselves to that, and yet there I was being drawn into, indeed forced into, doing it because of my gambling.

If you are suffering or have suffered in the same way as Tom, and hate the person that your gambling has created, then anchor that hatred of the industry and use it against them by never gambling again.

To help strengthen your resolve, you might find it a useful exercise to visualize the gambling industry getting rich at your expense. Industry profits may dwindle a little when times are tough, but the bulk tend to remain, while you may wonder where next month's mortgage is going to come from. Get passionate about that. Tell yourself that not one company will ever get a single pound from you again and carry this list around in your pocket or wallet.

Why don't you take the above list and keep it in a pocket. If you ever should have a gambling urge, take it out, read it and then picture these company profits, to which you are in effect contributing with your inevitable losses if you do go ahead and gamble again. What, you might win £1,000 today? That's hardly going to cripple companies worth as much as the above. Anyway they know, you know, and I certainly know, that any winnings won't actually stay with you. If not today, then tomorrow; if not tomorrow, then next month – but as sure as the sun sets every evening, you'll give that money back to them. They won't exactly be waiting until you do, to be able to pay the car insurance or the minimum payment on their maxed-out credit cards, so please don't lose sleep worrying about them!

While I've exaggerated a little here for dramatic effect, I believe the core of what I say to be true. The gambling industry would not be able to exist without your kind and charitable donations. The good news is that you no longer have to contribute to the maintenance of this cause. You never have to give these companies another penny of your hard-earned cash. That way, you'll be the winner every day – within your world, which is all you need to be concerned about.

Recap

1 Go out and research the profits of the companies you bet with.
2 List everything you've gone without this past year because of your gambling.
3 Keep a list of betting companies and their profits, and remember that big companies will benefit at your expense if you gamble again.

12

Cruel facts about a cruel industry

Much gambling involves animals, and so you might like now to consider how horses and dogs are treated as part of this industry. There is no doubt that, while they continue to be useful to their owners, many are treated well, albeit in an unnatural way. However there are serious abuses and once the animals have outlived their usefulness, many are treated as a commodity to be simply got rid of.

While compulsively gambling, the gambler may be oblivious to – or ignorant of – the full scale of what goes on in the gambling industry with regard to animal welfare. This chapter asks you to pause and give some thought to the living creatures who may go through misery and early deaths for the gambler's gratification, or to feed his vain hope of financial reward.

Horse racing

This is supposedly the proud 'Sport of Kings'. Current (2008) estimates are that 5,000 horses and ponies in the UK end their days at the wrong end of a rifle barrel in a slaughterhouse before perhaps being turned into the *plat du jour* (dish of the day) somewhere in Europe or becoming animal feed and other products. Of those 5,000, 2,000 (over five per day on average) are estimated to be racehorses. Those are the ones that weren't fast enough. What about those that die on the racecourse? You may think that this doesn't happen that often. I would argue that it does and let the figures speak for themselves:

In the UK:

219 killed on UK race tracks in 466 days in 2007–8

Four killed at one single race meeting at Wincanton races on 19 March 2007

Three killed in one day at Newton Abbot races on 11 June 2007

Three killed in one day at Market Rasen races on 8 July 2007

Three killed in one day at Ludlow races on 6 February 2008

Three killed over a two-day meeting at Aintree races on 4–5 April 2008

In the USA:

An average of at least 1,000 deaths per year (3 per day) since 2003, but very poor records kept

261 deaths just in California in 2007

In Australia:

115 deaths in 2007

87 deaths from 1 Jan to 8 June 2008

In South Africa:

41 deaths in 2007

Of course these statistics are not something the industry is exactly proud of or displays openly.

Is there possibly something not a little wrong in a supposedly civilized society when we promote a 'sport' that has such results? Whenever we talk about animals in any sport or activity it is important to remember that the animals have no say in their destiny. Racehorses have absolutely no choice in the matter. They don't choose whether they race or not. And although they may be well looked after when it suits the owners, we should also bear in mind that modern racehorses are highly bred for certain characteristics that many people believe make them far less contented than other horses (although these too are of course bred for the tasks we wish them to do!).

Greyhound racing

Over 10,000 greyhounds are retired each year, of which fewer than 3,000 are looked after by the Retired Greyhounds Trust. That leaves anything up to 7,000 per year being kept by owners or trainers, or in most cases abandoned or killed (sometimes illegally). Very few greyhounds race past the age of three. If we take an average lifespan to be 15 years, in the 12 years between a greyhound retiring and naturally dying, at least another 84,000 will be abandoned.

The RSPCA say that 12,000 greyhounds 'disappear' every year, but that is probably less than half the real number. Those 12,000 are the ones registered by the National Greyhound Racing Club (NGRC), as they need to be to race on registered tracks. Since most greyhounds finish racing before they are four years old (if they haven't already been shot, or even put to death by more cruel 'amateur' methods), they ought to be able to expect another ten years of healthy, peaceful living after their racing days are over. An owner who races dogs for money often cannot afford to keep the ever-increasing number of retired dogs, so paying a dog-killer perhaps £10 a head to shoot a metal bar through each dog's head to smash its skull is a cheap option. Every track and everyone concerned with greyhounds knows this goes on and accepts it. Why shouldn't they when greyhound racing brings in over £2 billion of betting revenue every year?

In addition to the 12,000 mentioned above, far more puppies are born and bred than are either needed in the industry or can fulfil their duties as racers. These too are slaughtered. That is done before registration takes place so they don't even appear on the radar screen. A registered greyhound charity, Greyhound Action (see Useful Addresses), estimates that at least 20,000 out of the 28,500 greyhounds bred annually to supply the British greyhound racing industry are destroyed each year.

Some calls for action were heard after a *Sunday Times* exposé of the industry in July 2006, but little has been done – perhaps the gambling industry is too powerful in this area?

So to finish, why did I write this chapter? Was it to attack the horse and dog racing industry? No, not at all, as I care nothing about them. I wrote it because I think all gamblers should be fully aware of the actions of the industry that depends on their money. It surely can't hurt to inform yourself more fully and it might help you give up!

For the views and research of animal welfare charities in this area I can recommend <www.greyhoundaction.org.uk> and <www.animalaid.org.uk>.

Recap

1 If greyhound or horse racing was your 'preferred' type of gambling, then recognize and accept the cruelty that can be involved in these industries.

2 Weigh up the consequences of your involvement in betting on animals. Can you justify it?

13

Life after gambling

For me, there was never any 'light switch' moment where I said 'I've stopped gambling and life is great.' Recovery from gambling is a gradual process, and the burden of guilt may take a long time to cast off completely. While you may find it helpful to see your addiction as an illness, you may not feel that this viewpoint totally absolves you from your actions in the past. You may still feel remorse for not being strong enough in the early days of your gambling to recognize what was going on in your life. You may wonder how you could have spent so much time in the twilight of the gambling coma, or you may grieve for the months and years during which your children were growing up half-noticed while your attention was elsewhere.

Coming out of the gambling coma takes time, and guilt is a very understandable part of the process. But as you progress, the benefits should become more obvious as you become better able to cope with normal, everyday life, regaining a little more energy and vigour. The following are some tips to help the process along:

- Don't beat yourself up. Think of yourself as basically a good person who was led astray through ignorance, or who contracted an illness. Focus on how you are overcoming the problem – mending your relationships, paying your debts, taking care of yourself and your family. Write down the positive aspects of your character, your strengths and achievements.
- Try to look after yourself physically a little better. The chances are that gambling led you into a sedentary life, with hours crouched over a computer, or over your winnings – or rather losings – in a casino. Take time out for a walk, go for a swim, join an exercise class – whatever works for you.
- Better sleep also helps. A calmer mind is an excellent soporific, but, in addition, practise good sleep hygiene. Drink less (or no)

caffeine after lunchtime; consume only a moderate amount of (or no) alcohol in the evenings; make your bedroom a pleasant, relaxing environment; and allow yourself sufficient time to wind down in the evening before you go to bed.

- Relax. Gambling is a stressful way of life, and it can be hard to wind down once you're used to spending hours each week keyed up. Try exercise, yoga or meditation
- Try to start liking yourself a little more. Give yourself inexpensive treats, such as listening to music you like (see Chapter 7), reading something you enjoy or chatting with a friend.
- Enjoy your money. It isn't the role of this book to give financial advice, and there are many sources of expert help on how to sort out debt if you do need this (see Useful addresses). However, once your finances are stabilized, there is less stress, and you can begin to enjoy money in a healthy way again. More importantly, every little bit of extra cash that is left over is clean money. It's clean in the sense that it is there because of good, hard, honest toil, not because it's been won off another person or institution. Gambling money, won or lost, is never clean. Because the extra cash is clean, what you choose to do with that money is clean. For once, you're not buying 'emotional credits'. It doesn't have to be spent as recompense for a past loss, or to guard against a future loss. There are no questions asked or thought as to how yesterday there was nothing in the kitty, and today it's overflowing! It's spent because it's spent!

I relay the following story, not out of arrogance or to show off, but to offer you hope and at the same time show you how much you miss out on while in the grip of compulsive gambling. I hope that you can achieve a similar time out from your gambling, or if you are already on the way of your new gambling-free life, can further appreciate how beautiful life can be now that you are free from gambling's clutches.

Two years on from my 'Release' we were in California taking a short break. We had rented a sporty little convertible and had enormous fun driving it up the mountains to Lake Tahoe on the California/Nevada border. I had been there previously, during my addiction, principally to gamble, but now I had the time, and more importantly the mental energy, to really breathe in and appreciate the stunning beauty of my surroundings. In many ways it was another moment of revelation, one which made it even more impossible for me ever to waste another second (or pound) gambling.

Having settled into our hotel room, without the previous sickening nervousness in the pit of my stomach as to whether my credit card would be accepted, we bought the makings of a fine but simple picnic and drove casually around the huge Lake Tahoe. Though it was mid May, the mountains were still capped with snow and the sheer beauty of our surroundings was breathtaking. Setting out our picnic on the sandy lake shore, we passed a glorious, relaxed two hours enjoying the birds, wildlife and, most of all, each other's company, something that would have been almost impossible during my gambling days. My mind was as clear as the crisp mountain air, my thoughts as deep as the blue of the lake water and my soul danced with unimpeded happiness. This was living!

Two hours later, and for the purposes of researching this book, we strolled into one of the biggest casinos in Lake Tahoe. The beautiful, natural light of the lakeside was replaced by a jungle of blaring neon. The still silence that allowed us to hear every note of the blue jay's call was now drowned by a cacophony of bells, sirens and supposedly enticing wails as the slots pleaded with us to entertain them. We sat at the bar drinking a couple of over-iced margaritas as we studied the bedlam before us. We looked at people's faces, struggling to find happiness or, at the very least, to see the reason why they were here and not outside enjoying such natural beauty for free. A young, pregnant girl was connected to a slot machine by what we at once described as a 'reverse umbilical cord'. It was in fact her gaming card, connected by a flexible leash to her belt, but it was as though it was sucking the life from her, rather than bringing life into her body.

At the other end of the casino and the other end of the age spectrum, we saw an aged pensioner being wheeled into the casino, oxygen cylinder by his side. Was he happy? Perhaps he was a veteran of foreign wars. Who knew? Who cared? Did the casino owners? Was this really how he wanted to spend his golden years?

While we were in the casino, my wife wanted to try to grasp just an inkling of what it was that had destroyed our lives for the past ten years, and so I taught her blackjack. She sat at the table and played $5 games with $60. If she won, the stake and the winnings would go to an animal shelter we had passed that morning. If we lost, the stake would go to the same place, so either way the shelter won. The $60 lasted just seven minutes, not because she was a bad player – both I and the croupier were advising her – but that was simply how the cards were turning. She hit one blackjack and so, at the end, gave me the $2.50 chip as a memento. I still have it to this day, alongside my special chip (see Chapter 8).

We walked out of that casino disheartened and dispirited. Not because we lost, but because we had witnessed such hidden sadness and desperation in there. There wasn't genuine fun and laughter, just dull, listless concentration and pleading eyes. Nonetheless, I regard that as the only time in my life that I ever walked away from gambling as a true winner.

Please go from here. Have a long, hard, considered think and go and find your own friends, those you mentally left behind, so long ago, when gambling took hold of you. I won't say good luck, because you and I don't believe in luck any more, but I sincerely hope that this book helps you go forward from this day and begin enjoying life again:

GAMBLING FREE!

'It is never safe to look into the future with eyes of fear.'

Edward H. Harriman

Appendix

My gambling history

(To be adapted to your own circumstances. This can only begin to help you, and more importantly those closest to you, if you are totally honest. This is a made-up example.)

Growing up and school days
My first memory of 'gambling' is of the 'penny falls' machines and the mechanical horse race machines on Blackpool pier as a child of 7 to 8 or so on summer holidays with my aunt and uncle. Maybe it was harmless fun, or maybe it sowed the seed that was later to become my addiction.

At age 16 to 17 I would occasionally go into a bookmaker's and place small bets on dogs or horses. Once I started drinking in pubs I would occasionally play on the slot machines, but it was certainly not problematic at this stage.

1981–84. University
The group of friends I shared a house with would often bet on the Saturday morning greyhounds and occasionally go to the local dog track for a night out. At this stage gambling still seemed to be fun and sociable and not something to worry about, although I did notice that I would sometimes go to the bookmakers by myself.

Estimated amount lost gambling during this period: £300

Dec 1984–Feb 1986. Assistant manager, The White Hart Pub and Restaurant, London
This was where I began recognizing that my gambling could get out of control. Doing split shifts, as is normal in pub/restaurant operations, I would often have three or so hours to kill in the afternoon between the lunchtime and evening shifts. It wasn't worth going home, so the bookie's and the casino in town offered me a warm place to go where I could switch off from work and 'enjoy' the chance of supplementing my salary through gambling. Several times I spent an entire week's wage packet in an afternoon.

Estimated amount lost gambling during this period: £20,000

Mar 1986–Nov 1990. Food and beverage manager, The Hanson Towers Hotel, London
During this period I began visiting casinos more and more often. I think that because weekends were busy and because of my shift patterns, I needed the comfort and 'action' of a casino midweek, as I was often unable to go out with friends during the weekend through work commitments. This turned me more and more into a loner who was seduced by the 'gloss' of the casinos and the welcome I would receive as a 'regular'. Work began to suffer as I sometimes stayed in the casino until three in the morning or later before going home, so I was always tired at work. As I got deeper and deeper into debt so I became more stressed, and so slept even less.

Estimated amount lost gambling during this period: £70,000

Jan 91–Dec 97. Assistant manager, El Citadel Hotel, Spain
The move abroad did me good and gave me breathing space from my gambling. I wasn't comfortable trying to gamble in a foreign country, and I avoided the lottery as I was sure I needed to be a Spanish citizen. If you know yourself well enough, and can 'manufacture' a move abroad, *sometimes* it can work in stopping your gambling. The problem now is that the internet follows you everywhere you go, so you will have access to internet casinos in virtually every country.

Estimated amount lost gambling during this period (on occasional visits back to the UK): £500

Feb 98–May 2006. Manager, Butlers Executive Dining, Sunrise Insurance Head Office, London
Having got married, we moved back to the UK to start our new life together. Having gone virtually six years without any real gambling while in Spain, I felt confident that whatever problems I'd had in the past were behind me, and I could go back to enjoying a day at the races, night at the casino and a few bets in the bookie's on a Saturday afternoon. I was *wrong*. Almost from the minute I placed my first bet, I was straight back into the trouble I was in

before – uncontrolled compulsive gambling. Within three months the 'nest egg' saved from Spain was blown and every month became a struggle to pay the mortgage and bills, let alone afford any holidays or luxuries. I lied more and more to my wife, and to make matters worse I started on internet gambling. I applied and was given more and more credit cards, all of which I maxed out on the internet sites until we were £50,000 in debt. At which point my wife left me. In my depression I gambled more, and drank more, until inevitably I lost my job.

Estimated amount lost gambling during this period: £200,000

Aug 07–present day. Countless assistant chef and dishwashing jobs in pubs and restaurants
I gamble virtually every pound I earn and live in a bedsit. Several times I've slept in shelters for the homeless and even out on the streets.

Sample covering letter to be sent with your gambling history

Dear [insert recipient's name]
By now, after our phone call the other day/night, you'll know that I am a compulsive gambler who for the past . . . years has been addicted to gambling. It has completely ruined my life but more importantly it has ruined [insert the name of your partner/spouse if you have one]. That is a burden that I will carry for the rest of my life. I don't expect you to understand how I could do this, but please try and accept that I was sick in the way that any addict is sick.

I have lied all this time to you and have borrowed money from you under false pretences. For all of that and for all of the pain I have caused you, and will cause you through you knowing this, I am truly sorry.

I have included my gambling history so that you can at last finally know the truth of how bad it was and when were the worst periods. For once in my life I am trying to be honest. I have embarked on a system known as Gamblers Aloud and I have managed . . . days/ months without a gamble, and I am feeling a little better about the future. Their philosophy is to get the problem out in the open as much as possible. I know it will be a struggle, but I am determined to turn my life around. It might help you understand a little more about the addiction if you read the book part of the system, which is called *Overcoming Gambling* by Philip Mawer (a former compulsive gambler) and is aimed not just at compulsive gamblers but all those affected by their gambling.

If you can find it in your heart to help me, then that would be fantastic and mean the world to me, but what is more important is that you try and help [insert the name of your partner/spouse if you have one] as he/she is the victim in all this.

Once again, I am so sorry for all of this.

Love

Sample exclusion letter to an internet casino

Many casinos operate a voluntary self-exclusion policy which effectively allows you to ban yourself from gambling there for a specified period of time, often from between six months to five years. The Gambling Act 2005 makes provisions for individual company self-exclusion, but there is to date no effective coordinated national scheme, so that you may need to contact operators on an individual basis. You may need to provide personal information such as your name, address, telephone number, and distinguishing physical characteristics such as height, build, hair and eye colour, along with relevant ID such as a driving licence. You may also need to provide a photo of yourself so that staff can identify you if you do set foot on the premises. These schemes aren't necessarily foolproof, but they do provide a helpful starting point in terms of demonstrating your commitment to giving up gambling.

Alternatively, if the casinos you frequented don't operate such a policy, you could simply write to them, including all the information outlined above.

Useful addresses and references

Useful addresses

General

CNWL Soho Treatment Centre
Fourth Floor, Soho Centre for Health
1 Frith Street
London W1D 3HZ
Tel.: 020 7534 6699
Website: www.cnwl.nhs.uk/gambling.html

The Centre houses the National Problem Gambling Clinic, whose services may be accessed via phone or the website.

Gam-Anon
Helpline: 08700 50 88 80
Website: www.gamanon.org.uk

For families and friends of problem gamblers.

Gamble Aware
RIGT
10 Brick Street
London W1J 7HQ
Helpline: 0845 6000 133 (run by **GamCare**: see below)
Website: www.gambleaware.co.uk

Helps the individual notice signs that gambling may be a problem.

Gamblers Aloud
Website: www.gamblersaloud.com

Gamblers Anonymous
C/o CVS Building
5 Trafford Court
Off Trafford Way
Doncaster DN1 1PN
National Helpline: 020 7384 3040
Website: www.gamblersanonymous.org.uk

A nationwide organization to help problem gamblers. The website gives details of meetings around the country, also of the online forum and chat rooms available.

GamCare
Second Floor
7–11 St John's Hill
London SW11 1TR
Tel.: 020 7801 7000
National Helpline: 0845 6000 133
Website: www.gamcare.org.uk

Provides information, confidential advice and emotional support to
anyone suffering through a gambling problem. A team of advisers runs
the helpline from 8 a.m. daily.

Gambling Commission
Victoria Square House
Victoria Square
Birmingham B2 4BP
Tel.: 0121 230 6666
Website: www.gamblingcommission.gov.uk

An independent public body sponsored by the Department of Culture,
Media and Sport and set up in 2005 to regulate commercial gambling in
Britain.

RCA Trust
Mirren House
Back Sneddon Street
Paisley PA3 2AF
Tel.: 0141 887 0880
Website: www.rcatrust.org.uk

Helps people who have addiction problems, including gambling, and their
families and friends. The website includes details of access counselling for
people with sensory impairment.

Responsible Gambling Council (Canada)
Website: www.responsiblegambling.org

An independent non-profit organization committed to problem gambling
prevention.

Charities

Animal Aid
The Old Chapel
Bradford Street
Tonbridge TN9 1AW
Tel.: 01732 366533
Website: www.animalaid.org.uk

Greatwood
Rainscombe Hill Farm
Clench Common
Marlborough
Wiltshire SN8 4DT
Tel.: 01672 514535
Website: www.racehorsesgreatwood.org.

A racehorse welfare charity, Greatwood provides futures for former racehorses and help for children with special educational needs through their interaction in unique programmes of rehabilitation and education.

Greyhound Action
Website: www.greyhoundaction.org.uk

An independent group campaigning against the inherent cruelty of the greyhound racing industry.

Greyhound Rescue
Website: www.greyhoundrescue.co.uk

Dedicated to the rescue and rehabilitation of abused and abandoned greyhounds.

Homing Ex-Racehorses Organisation Scheme (HEROS)
Website: www.heroscharity.org

RSPCA
Tel.: 0300 1234 555 (advice and information)
     0300 1234 999 (to report cruelty)

Counselling

British Association of Counselling and Psychotherapy
BACP House
15 St John's Business Park
Lutterworth
Leics LE17 4HB
Tel.: 01455 883300
Website: www.bacp.co.uk

Debt advice

Consumer Credit Counselling Service
Wade House
Merrion Centre
Leeds LS2 8NG
Freephone: 0800 138 1111 (8 a.m. to 8 p.m., Monday to Friday)
Website: www.cccs.co.uk

Credit Action
Sixth Floor, Lynton House
7–12 Tavistock Square
London WC1H 9LT
Tel.: 020 7380 3390
Website: www.creditaction.org.uk

Provides assistance for those trying to avoid debt problems.

National Debtline
Tel.: 0808 808 4000
    0800 197 6026 (for businesses experiencing difficulties)
Website: www.nationaldebtline.co.uk

For free, confidential, independent advice on how to deal with debt problems, taking into account that debt law varies as to which part of the UK you live in.

UK Insolvency Helpline
Tel.: 0800 074 6918
Website: www.insolvencyhelpline.co.uk

Gives non-judgemental confidential advice on debt, Individual Voluntary Arrangements and bankruptcy.

References

Christensen, Margaret H., Patsdaughter, Carol A., and Babington, Lynn M. (2001), 'Health Care Providers' Experiences with Problem Gamblers', *Journal of Gambling Studies*, vol. 17, no. 1, pp. 71–9.
Rosenthal, Richard J., and Lorenz, Valerie C. (1992), *Psychiatric Clinics of North America*, vol. 15, no. 3, pp. 647–60.

Index

Page numbers in *italic* indicate figures and shaded boxes.

acceptance of loss 21–2
    learned helplessness 52
addiction approach to gambling
    18–23
affirmation making 84–5
Alcoholics Anonymous (AA) 39–40,
    89
anonymity 40
    versus the Gamblers Aloud
    approach 39–44

bank statements 58–60
bracketing 26
brain research *47*
British Medical Association (BMA) 46

chips, use in recovery from gambling
    71–6
cognitive behavioural therapy (CBT)
    46
coin tossing 72–3
compassion 33, 75, 86, 87, 89, 90
competitiveness 20–1
confrontation 3–4, 24–6, *25*, 28–31
    preparation 28–30
    see also release from problem
    gambling
conscience
    guilt 11, 24, 30, 33, 49–50, 68,
    102
    maturing your conscience 69–70
control 73–4
    see also helplessness
credit card statements 58–60

dangers of gambling
    contemplating the futility and
    77–84
    see also health effects of gambling;
    mental health
desperation phase of gambling 16–17
dignity 68–9

emotional zone of gambling
    addiction to the twilight zone
    20–3
    emotional solitary confinement
    50–1
    negative emotions 4–5, 49
    state of neutral emotion 51
exclusion letter 109
exercise 36–7
    the mind gym *64*

futility of gambling 77–84

Gamblers Aloud (and allowed)
    approach 39–44
    'Just for today,' adaptation 89–90
    see also recovery from problem
    gambling; release from problem
    gambling
Gamblers Anonymous (GA) 39–40,
    41–2, 89
    checklist for deciding if you have a
    gambling problem 1–2
gamblers' fallacy 73
gamblers' loved ones 3–5, 6
    money and 4–5, 59–60, 83
    as part of an intervention team
    24–6, 33
    remorse for pain caused to 49
Gambling Act (2005) 109
'Gambling addiction and its
    treatment within the NHS' 46
gambling as an illness 46–55
    acceptance of 47–8
    assessing your health 54
    effects on physical health 52–4, 84
    effects on the brain *47*
    emotional effects of 50–1
    learned helplessness 52
    responsibility, guilt and 49–50
    suicide rate for gambling addicts
    25

'symptoms'/practical effects of 49,
    52–4
    see also emotional zone of
        gambling
gambling history 31–3, 57–8
    example 106–8
    sample covering letter 108–9
gambling industry 15, 21, 46, 78
    cruel facts 98–100
    hatred for 70, 94–7
    profits 95–7
gambling origins 71
gambling urges 62–4
Greyhound Action 100
greyhound racing, the cruel facts
    99–100
guilt 11, 24, 30, 33, 49–50, 68, 102

habit breaking 18–23
    see also release from problem
        gambling
health effects of gambling 52–4, 84
    assessing your health 54
    on the brain 47
    loss of sleep 52, 53, 84
    see also mental health
health professionals 10
healthy life style 102–4
    see also exercise
helplessness
    learned 52
    phase of gambling 17
horse racing, the cruel facts 98–9
humility 41, 70, 79, 86, 90
    Tree of Humility 90–3, 91

'Just for today,' adapted for Gamblers
    Aloud 89–90

Ladder of Life exercise 6–8, 7, 8
learned helplessness 52
life after gambling 102–5
listening 26
losing phase of gambling 15–16
luck 74–5
lying 4, 40, 57, 83

mental health
    effects of gambling on the brain 47

health professionals and mental
    illness 10
the mind gym 64
suicide rate for gambling addicts
    25
    see also emotional zone of
        gambling
money
    and competitiveness 20–1
    cutting access to finances 66–8
    and deceit/treatment of loved ones
        4–5, 59–60, 83
    and the gambling industry 15, 46,
        94–7
    importance of 75
    new relationship with 86–7
    and the reminder chip 74
    signposts 58–60
    see also emotional zone of
        gambling; problem gambling
        phases
music 42–3

Narcotics Anonymous (NA) 39–40
neural affects of gambling 47
NHS treatments for problem
    gambling 46

Parkinson's disease 54
pleasure and pain principle 9
preparing to stop gambling 5–10
problem gambling phases
    desperation 16–17
    helplessness 17
    losing 15–16
    winning 14–15
problem gambling recovery (staying
    stopped) see recovery from
    problem gambling
problem gambling release see release
    from problem gambling
problem gambling signs
    checklist for gamblers 1–2
    checklist for partners or friends
        2–3
procrastination 9–10

readiness to stop gambling 1–12
recovery from problem gambling

accepting gambling as an illness
47–9
anchoring your hatred of the
gambling industry 70, 94–7
changing the 'just for today'
approach 89–90
contemplating the futility and
danger of gambling 77–85
dealing with urges 62–4
helping others and building your
own 87–9
importance of humility and
compassion in 86–93
restoring dignity and self-respect
66–76
and the route of cutting access to
finances 66–8
signpost of accepting you were a
helpless gambler 62
signpost of your bank statements
and credit card bills 58–60
signpost of your gambling history
57–8
signpost of your lost time 60–1
taking responsibility 49–50
using emotional solitary
confinement 51
using the prop of the chip 71–6
see also gambling as an illness
relapse prevention see recovery from
problem gambling
relationships with gamblers 3–5, 6
see also gamblers' loved ones
relaxation 103
smoking and 21–2
release from problem gambling
adopting alternatives to gambling
36–8, 42–3
breaking the fear and mythology
of gambling 18–23
choosing who to work with 24–6
creating your rock bottom 26–38
and the Gamblers Aloud approach
39–44

self-exclusion 35–6
step 1: preparing for confrontation
or confession 28–30
step 2: getting the truth into the
open 30–1
step 3: writing your gambling
history 31–3, 106–9
step 4: saying goodbye 33–6
step 5: breaking up your behaviour
pattern and routines 36–8
taking up exercise 36–7
'Team CG' 32–3
using the power of music 42–3
see also recovery from problem
gambling
responsibility 49–50
rock bottom
creation 16–17, 26–38
myth 25
RSPCA 100

self-exclusion programmes 35–6
sample letter 109
self-respect 68–70
Seligman, Martin 52
sex, loss of interest in 84
signs of problem gambling 1–3
sleep 52, 53, 84, 102–3
smoking, addiction comparison to
gambling 18–19, 21–2
Soho Problem Gambling Clinic 46
suicide 10, 25
support team 24–6, 33

'Team CG' 32–3
see also support team
therapeutic interventions 25
time, as a precious commodity 60–1
twilight zone of gambling see
emotional zone of gambling

urges, handling of 62–4

winning phase of gambling 14–15